ENGINEERING a SOLID RETIREMENT

Build a plan, structure income and prosper.

Jeremy D. North

This book discusses general concepts for retirement planning, and is not intended to provide tax or legal advice. Individuals are urged to consult with their tax and legal professionals regarding these issues. It is important to know a) that annuities and some of their features have costs associated with them; b) that annuities used to fund IRAs do not afford any additional measure of tax deferral for the IRA owner; c) that income received from annuities and securities may be taxable; and d) that securities' past performance does not influence or predict future results.

Copyright © 2017 by Gradient Positioning Systems, LLC. All rights reserved. No part of this publication may be reproduced, distributed, or transmitted in any form or by any means, electronic or mechanical, including photocopying, recording, or by any information storage and retrieval system, without written permission of the publisher, except in the case of brief quotations embodied in critical reviews and certain other noncommercial uses permitted by copyright law.

Printed in the United States of America

First Printing, 2018

Gradient Positioning Systems, LLC
4105 Lexington Avenue North, Suite 110
Arden Hills, MN 55126
(877) 901-0894

Contributors: Nick Stovall, Mike Binger, Nate Lucius and Gradient Positioning Systems, LLC.

Gradient Positioning Systems, LLC and Jeremy D. North are not affiliated with or endorsed by the Social Security Administration or any government agency.

This publication contains the opinions and ideas of its author. It is intended to provide helpful and informative material on the subject matter covered. It is sold with the understanding that the author and publisher are not engaged in rendering professional services in the book. The information provided is not intended as tax, investment or legal advice, and should not be relied on as such. If the reader requires personal assistance or advice, you are encouraged to seek tax, investment or legal advice from an independent professional advisor.

The author and publisher specifically disclaim any responsibility for any liability, loss, or risk, personal or otherwise, which is incurred as a consequence, directly or indirectly, of the use and application of any of the contents of this book.

Trademarks: All terms mentioned in this book that are known to be or are suspected of being trademarks or service marks have been appropriately capitalized. The publisher cannot attest to the accuracy of this information. Use of a term in this book should not be regarded as affecting the validity of any trademark or service mark.

This book provides general information that is intended, but not guaranteed, to be correct and up-to-date information on the subjects discussed, and should not be regarded as a complete analysis of these subjects. You should not rely on statements or representations made within the book or by any externally referenced sources. No party assumes liability for any loss or damage resulting from errors or omissions or reliance on or use of this material.

The contents of this book should not be taken as financial advice, or as an offer to buy or sell any securities, fund, or financial instruments. Any illustrations or situations presented are hypothetical and do not take into account your particular investment objectives, financial situation or needs and are not suitable for all persons. Any investments and/or investment strategies mentioned involve risk including the possible loss of principal. There is no assurance that any investment strategy will achieve its objectives. No portion of the content should be construed as an offer or solicitation for the purchase or sale of any security. Any insurance products mentioned are guaranteed by the claims paying ability of the issuer and certain limitations and expenses may apply. The contents of this book should not be taken as an endorsement or recommendation of any particular company or individual, and no responsibility can be taken for inaccuracies, omissions, or errors

The author does not assume any responsibility for actions or non-actions taken by people who have read this book, and no one shall be entitled to a claim for detrimental reliance based upon any information provided or expressed herein. Your use of any information provided does not constitute any type of contractual relationship between yourself and the provider(s) of this information. The author hereby disclaims all responsibility and liability for all use of any information provided in this book. The materials here are not to be interpreted as establishing an attorney-client or any other relationship between the reader and the author or his firm.

Although great effort has been expended to ensure that only the most meaningful resources are referenced in these pages, the author does not endorse, guarantee, or warranty the accuracy reliability, or thoroughness of any referenced information, product, or service. Any opinions, advice, statements, services, offers, or other information or content expressed or made available by third parties are those of the author(s) or publisher(s) alone. References to other sources of information does not constitute a referral, endorsement, or recommendation of any product or service. The existence of any particular reference is simply intended to imply potential interest to the reader.

The views expressed herein are exclusively those of the author and do not represent the views of any other person or any organization with which the author is, or may be associated.

TABLE OF CONTENTS

INTRODUCTION 1

CHAPTER 1: ORGANIZING YOUR ASSETS 9

CHAPTER 2: TRUE DIVERSIFICATION 25

CHAPTER 3: INCOME: GETTING IT TOGETHER 41

CHAPTER 4: OPTIMIZING SOCIAL SECURITY 47

CHAPTER 5: FILLING THE INCOME GAP 67

CHAPTER 6: THE HOUSE MADE OF CARDS:
A WRONG WAY TO INVEST DURING
RETIREMENT 81

CHAPTER 7: THE HOUSE MADE OF BRICKS:
TACTICAL MONEY MANAGEMENT 95

CHAPTER 8: THE THREE PILLARS OF INVESTING:
LIQUIDITY, SAFETY AND RETURN 109

CHAPTER 9: TAX PLANNING DURING RETIREMENT 115

CHAPTER 10: THE FUTURE OF U.S. TAXATION 129

CHAPTER 11: THE FUTURE OF YOUR TAXATION 145

CHAPTER 12: YOUR LEGACY BEYOND DOLLARS
AND CENTS 153

CHAPTER 13: PREPARING YOUR LEGACY 163

CHAPTER 14: FINDING A FINANCIAL PROFESSIONAL
WHO HAS INTEGRITY 177

GLOSSARY 193

INTRODUCTION

"Engineers turn dreams into reality."
– Hayao Miyazaki

Roger and Emily are one year into their retirement. They have worked hard, saved diligently and managed to build a nest egg worth just over $2 million. But they are afraid to spend it.

Emily wants to travel, maybe visit Europe and take the grandkids to see the ocean. But Roger has told her that they can't afford to spend one single penny. He says they have to be careful with this money in order to make sure it will last. Although she understands this, Emily is feeling miserable. It doesn't seem fair to have worked so hard and come this far only to still be worried about pinching pennies.

Meanwhile, Roger has been closely watching the stock market. He saw what happened in 2001 and then again in 2008 when their portfolio tanked by 42 percent. He also saw what a rocky year 2015 was on Wall Street, and he knows they have to be ready. Not only do *they have to watch out for market risk, but there is also a good chance that he or Emily might get sick and see an increase to their health care costs as they get older. He knows that Emily wants to travel, but he doesn't know how long they will live, how long this money has to last or what the future holds.*

Roger and Emily are finally retired, but they aren't enjoying it. This isn't at all what they hoped for when they dreamed about their golden years.

Many retirees like Roger and Emily have problems on their mind that are preventing them from enjoying retirement. You, like them, might also be afraid of running out of money, worried about taking on too much risk, and concerned health care costs will affect the money you need to live on during retirement. You're not crazy for feeling this way. Retirement planning has gotten much harder, and more of the responsibility has been placed in the hands of the individual. Defined-contribution plans such as the 401(k) plan have replaced defined-benefit pensions, our stock market has entered into a global economy, and people are living much longer than they used to. When you take into account all of the different components that can affect the quality of your retirement—market risk, inflation, Social Security and tax law just to name a few—then you can see how these working parts are like an engine. Instead of running a car, you want to power your lifestyle. How do you get all of these different components, IRAs, investments and benefits to work together efficiently so that you don't run out of money?

One of the principles of engineering states that the fewer the working parts, the less likely something will go wrong. Unfortunately, as a retiree today, there's no way to avoid the complexity of many moving parts. But there is good news: many helpful strategies, products and investment options are out there that

INTRODUCTION

you might not be aware of, and they can work in your favor to improve your financial plan with peace of mind. **You don't have to spend your retirement planning to lose the money you've worked so hard to save.** Instead of worrying about rates of return and the conditions on Wall Street, you can choose instead to focus on the design of a holistic plan that utilizes *strategy* to deliver financial comfort and, more importantly, peace of mind.

As an independent investment advisor with multiple engineering bachelor's degrees and a master's degree, I have a passion for helping people and retirees graduate to a more strategic level of money management. The 360-degree approach advocated by my firm and outlined in this book takes the macro-view when planning to look at the next 20 to 30 years of your life with an eye for both short-term and long-term risks. By carefully engineering a plan, we can get all the different components of investments, taxes and lifestyle managed efficiently and working together. This frees you from the obligation of having to *worry*. Instead, you can do what you're supposed to do during retirement: *enjoying life*.

CONGRATULATIONS, YOU MADE IT. NOW WHAT?

Most people who come to me to talk about their retirement have done a good job saving up to this point in their life. I take a look at their assets, and I say to them, "Congratulations, you made it. You've arrived." The problem is that some don't believe me. Instead of taking the next step to **secure** their retirement income and design a lower risk investment plan, they want to keep relying on the stock market with the same stock-bond portfolio.

Retirement represents a new and different phase of your financial life. It is quite unlike any financial challenge you have ever faced before, which brings us to the first big mistake you can make as a retiree today: **relying on your investment portfolio as the basis for an income plan.** Most Americans today can rely on their Social Security as the base of an income plan, but it's your investments which make up the difference between the money you know you have for income, and the money you need. Without a pension to rely on, most people turn to their investments using simplistic advice such as the 4-percent rule, and while those formulas might have worked in the past, times have changed. With market volatility at all-time highs and interest rates on typical safe money investments at all-time lows, today's retirees need a better strategy. With a plan, a process, and the guidance of a professional, you can take your collection of investments and turn them into a more safe and comfortable income producing retirement.

The second biggest mistake people make is thinking that their portfolio is diversified, when in reality, it's not. Sure you might have a lot of different stocks and funds in your portfolio, but variety is not the same thing as diversity. It's been my experience that the big brokerage firms put numerous different funds in your portfolio that all do the pretty much the same thing. When the market goes down, your portfolio goes down; whatever the S&P 500 does, your portfolio follows a similar pattern. In 2008 when the market dropped significantly, most people with brokerage firms lost a lot of money, which means unless you are doing something different today, when the market takes another turn, you could also experience a similar drop.

Theoretically, a diversified portfolio is supposed to spread out the risk, but in most of the portfolios I've seen, the diversification is not structured appropriately for someone entering retirement. All the funds are pointed in the same direction, which means even a "conservative" portfolio can lose considerably. Most people who feel they are conservative don't relish the idea of losing even 10 percent, much less 30 percent or more like in 2008, as they go into retirement. Chapter 2 shows you what true diversification looks like and why as a retiree, *your portfolio can earn higher returns*

INTRODUCTION

if you are less concerned about staying IN during the best days and more concerned about getting OUT during the worst days. Chapter 5 shows you how to get a guaranteed element to your income plan. Chapter 6 explains the Sequence of Returns and why getting negative returns in your portfolio during your retirement distribution years affects you worse than during your working years. Chapter 7 reveals how tactical money management can result in a superior portfolio.

Lastly, many investors going into retirement put way too much blind trust in the big brokerage firms that currently manage their money. It's easy to mistake glossy marketing material, celebrity endorsed TV commercials and ad campaigns for trustworthiness and excellence. It can also be hard to make a change when you're feeling comfortable. **But please be aware, folks, that NOT making a change in your investment strategy when your needs change near retirement can be the worst mistake of them all.** You've made it this far, and you've worked hard. So now what? I'm glad you asked.

WHAT YOUR BROKER IS NOT TELLING YOU

As you near or enter into retirement, you are leaving behind what we in the planning industry call *the accumulation phase*. These are your working years when earning and accumulating money are your main goals. You are earning an income from your job and putting money into investment accounts. Once you retire, however, all this changes. You are no longer earning a steady income, and no longer putting money into your retirement plans. Instead, you are taking money OUT of those plans in order to replace your income. This "taking money out" is what we in the planning industry call *the distribution phase*, and it necessitates the crafting of an efficient and well-designed plan in order to ensure your dollars last as long as you want them to.

The tactics you relied on when investing during your accumulation years need to change once you get near the distribution phase of life. Your broker isn't likely going to tell you this, because he or she has a vested interest in getting you to keep your money with him or her. They don't earn commissions by helping people to optimize their Social Security or design an income plan; they make money by selling accumulation investments. Accumulation investments aren't bad—they do have their place in a distribution plan—but they aren't the only strategy you need. To use a Mc Donald's metaphor, you might think of brokerage firms as the "Big Macs" of the investment world. Sure they're available on nearly every major street corner, consumed by 20 year olds and 80 year olds alike and keep the basic masses of our population fed. But their ultimate goal is to increase their stock price and shareholder value, not provide high quality food in the best interest of the customer. Is that what you what really need at this critical point in your life? Your portfolio is about to undergo the biggest test of its life: it has to fuel the marathon of your distribution years. Do you really want to run a retirement on a fast-food mentality?

Just like eating at Mc Donald's won't make you skinny, going to a big brokerage firm alone won't make you fat with returns. To fuel a healthy body, you need a balanced meal; to fuel a retirement, you need a balanced portfolio. There are a variety of stronger options out there that when combined with tax planning and Social Security optimization, can result in a plan to free you from the worry of running out of money. When you work with an independent professional who specializes in distribution planning, he or she will take you through all four phases of the holistic process—Discovery, Strategy, Implementation and Monitoring/Adjusting. This process is described throughout the chapters of this book to address your financial situation from four perspectives: Income, Asset accumulation, Taxes and Legacy.

INTRODUCTION

YOUR FINANCIAL AND RETIREMENT GPS – A GUIDED PLANNING SYSTEM

Engineers have an aversion to uncertainty, which means we naturally thrive on challenges that allow us to calculate and build efficient, low-risk machines. This is why building retirement plans is so appealing to me, and why I am so passionate about what I do. Let me explain it another way using one of my favorite engineering quotes by Donno. He says that there are basically three kinds of people:
- Those who make wonders happen
- Those who watch wonders happen
- Those who wonder, *what the heck just happened?*

When it comes to retirement income, you want to work with the person who can make wonders happen so you don't end up being the person wondering what the heck just happened to a portfolio, travel plans, and dreams for a retirement.

At 360 IRA, we believe that one of the primary principals to make money during retirement is to avoid losing it in the first place. Our focus is on our clients, not shareholders, and structuring a comfortable stress-free retirement plan built for tax-efficiency and reduced-risk investment growth. Our mission is to be your last financial advisor, and your grandchildren's first. We go full-circle with our plans to make sure your portfolio can go the distance, which means we don't just put you in products and then walk away. We stay with you throughout your distribution years to monitor, adjust and make sure the engine of your plan continues to deliver the performance you deserve.

To that end, we feel the following services are necessary for today's retirees and should all be provided under one roof:
- Social Security Maximization
- Retirement Income Plan
- Investment Risk & Fee Analysis

- Portfolio Stress Testing
- Investment Management Strategies for Retirees
- Tax Planning
- Tax Return Reviews
- Lifestyle Protection Analysis
- Medicare Supplement Plan Assistance
- Prescription Drug Plan Assistance
- Beneficiary Audits
- Will and Trust Review

There is much more to building a solid plan than just riding the stock market roller coaster. You have the ability to get off the roller coaster and into a plan designed specifically for you. I personally invite you to sit down with our firm to find out how we can engineer a better retirement that's enjoyable for you.

— *Jeremy D. North*, President and Chief Financial Advisor at 360 Investment and Retirement Advisory.

1
ORGANIZING YOUR ASSETS

"One of the greatest discoveries a person makes, one of their great surprises, is to find they can do what they were afraid they couldn't do."
— Henry Ford

Will your Social Security benefit, savings and other retirement assets be enough? If you're like Mark and Kristi, you hope so. When the couple turned 60 years old, they started thinking about what their lives would be like in the next 10 years. When would they retire? What would their retirement look like? How much money did they have?

They could both count on Social Security benefits, but neither one really knew how much their monthly checks would be, or when to file for them. Mark had a modest pension that he could begin collecting *at age 67. He had always hoped to retire before that age. Kristi had a 401(k), but she honestly wasn't exactly sure how it worked, how she could draw money from it and how much income it would provide once she retired.*

While Mark and Kristi may sound like they're totally in the dark about their retirement, the truth is there are a lot of people just like them. They know retirement is coming and know they have some assets to rely on, but they aren't sure how it will all come together to provide them with a retirement income.

You spend your entire working life hoping what you put into your retirement accounts will help you live comfortably once you clock out of the workforce for good. The key word in that sentiment and the word that can make retirement feel like a looming problem instead of a rewarding life stage, is *hope*. You hope you'll have enough money.

Leaving your retirement up to chance is unadvisable by nearly any standard, yet millions of people find themselves hoping instead of planning for a happy ending. **Happy endings require more than hope; they need a focused and well-executed plan.** With information, tools and professional guidance, engineering a successful retirement plan can put you in control of your financial management.

WHAT DOES MONEY MEAN TO YOU?

Money represents more than the paper it's printed on. It is the embodiment of your time, your talents, and your commitments. It buys the food you eat, the house you sleep in, the car you drive, and the clothes you wear. It also helps provide you with the lifestyle you want to live once you retire.

You have spent a lifetime earning it, spending it, and hopefully, accumulating it. When the time comes for retirement, you want your money to provide you with a comfortable lifestyle and stable income after your working days are done. You might also have other desires, such as traveling, purchasing property, or moving to be closer to your family (or farther away). You may also want your assets to provide for your loved ones after you are gone.

The truth is that it takes more than just money to fulfill those needs and desires. Your income, your plans for retirement, your future healthcare expenses, and the continued accumulation of your assets after you stop working and drawing a paycheck all rely on one thing: *You.*

The way you approach your retirement impacts your income, the taxes your assets are subject to, your financial stability in the future, and your legacy. It is a truism among financial professionals that **one hour of organizing your assets can be worth more than an entire lifetime of working and saving** when it comes to retirement.

How is that possible? The fact of the matter is that after working and saving for a lifetime, entering retirement changes all of the rules you have known and followed for your entire career. Instead of an earning and saving paradigm, you are moving into an income and asset leveraging paradigm where you need to use the money you have earned and saved to generate income and preserve your assets for you. Making sure your assets last for your lifetime will depend on how you decide to invest them, and in what order you will spend them.

With forces like inflation, market volatility, and fluctuating interest rates working against you, knowing what to do with your assets has never been more important. And the difference between making a good decisions and a bad decision has never had such a dramatic impact on how people retire.

The question isn't CAN you or SHOULD you put your money to work for you and your family. It's HOW.

You have to understand what you want your money to do for you before you can figure out where to put it and how and when to take it out. The amount of money you've saved in your retirement accounts might be just a number to a broker, but really it represents much more. That's why when you sit down to talk with your financial professional about how to organize this money, the first conversation you have should be about you.

Where are you NOW, where do you want to GO, and what are the concerns or obstacles you have GETTING THERE?

You've worked a lifetime to get here to the point of retirement, but the period of time in front of you represents a financial challenge unlike any you've faced before. An investment advisor can't recommend a strategy until he or she first understands the kind of assets you have to work with, and what you are hoping to achieve. They also need to know about the kinds of things you are worried about, because priorities help dictate the direction of a plan. To that end, we will go through a thorough series of questions designed to get to know you. Expect questions to include the following:

- When do you want to retire?
- Do you love your job? Hate your job?
- If you want to retire early, what is preventing you?
- Are you planning to work part-time during retirement?
- Let's discuss family history and life expectancy?
- Do you have any health issues or concerns?
- Do you want to plan for long-term care expenses?
- Do you want to ensure a certain legacy amount for your beneficiaries?
- Do you have any hobbies, large projects or major expenses to build your retirement around?

Next, your financial professional will take a look at all the assets you have saved to see where and how you are currently positioned. Organizing your assets is a customized process, and every situation will be a little bit different, but most people feel a sense of relief when it's done. The things you didn't know become known, and the big problems or worries now have realistic solutions. There are even cases where planning ahead rewards you with the most priceless gift of all: *more time*. The sad truth is that the larger financial industry wants you to work longer, make more money, and spend less of your retirement savings. However, imagine if your investment advisor was able to show you a comprehensive written plan that revealed you could retire *now* instead of waiting five years? Wouldn't you want to at least know about it?

By running a series of reports and analysis (such as those discussed in Chapter 2), some financial professionals can take a look at all the many working parts that affect a retirement including inflation, market risk, taxes and long-term care costs. All of these different variables can be brought together into one plan, one binder customized for you, and organized on spreadsheets so you can SEE the numbers and KNOW what's possible. **Imagine what it would feel like to hold in your hands a written plan that shows you why you no longer have to worry about running out of money.** This is what you stand to gain by working with a financial professional who is a fiduciary dedicated to retirement planning and maximizing your lifestyle.

WILL YOU PLAN TO LOSE, OR PLAN TO LIVE?

Now that you know there's more to saving and planning for retirement than filing for your Social Security benefit and drawing income from your 401(k), you can begin to **create a strategy for your retirement** that can have a significant impact on your financial landscape after you stop drawing a paycheck. Understanding how to manage your assets entails risk management, risk diversification, tax planning and income planning preparation throughout your life stages. These strategies can help you leverage more from each one of the hard-earned dollars you set aside for your retirement. Working with a financial professional can help you determine your best course of action.

Advice about what to do with money has been around as long as money has existed. Hindsight allows us to see which advice was good and which advice didn't cut the mustard. Some sources of advice have been around for a very long time. While there are some basic investment concepts that have stood the test of time, most strategies that work adapt to changing conditions in the market, in the economy and the world, as well as changes in your personal circumstances.

The reality is that investment strategies and savings plans that worked in the past have encountered challenging new circumstances that have turned them on their heads. The Great Recession of the early 2000's highlighted how old investment ideas were not only ineffective but incredibly destructive to the retirement plans of millions of Americans. The threat of short-term risks such as market volatility and running out of income sent many retirees back to work after the housing crisis of 2008. Long-term risks such as inflation and the cost of long-term care have other people worried at night and unable to sleep.

Perhaps the most important lessons investors learned from the Great Recession is that not understanding where your money is invested (and the potential risks of those investments) can work against you, your plans for retirement and your legacy. Saving and investing money isn't enough to truly get the most out of it. You must have a planned approach to managing your assets.

Essentially, managing your money and investments so you can *enjoy* your retirement instead of *worry* about it is an ongoing process that requires customization and adaptation to a changing world. And make no mistake; the world is always changing. What worked for your parents or even your parents' parents was probably good advice back then. People in retirement or approaching retirement today need new ideas and professional guidance.

HOPE SO VS. KNOW SO MONEY

Let's take a look at some of the basic truths about money as it relates to saving for retirement.

There are essentially two kinds of money: *Hope So* and *Know So*. Everyone can divide their money into these two categories. Some have more of one kind than the other. The goal isn't to eliminate one kind of money but to balance them as you approach retirement.

Hope So Money is money that is at risk. It fluctuates with the market. It has no minimum guarantee. It is subject to investor activity, stock prices, market trends, buying trends, etc. You get the picture. This money is exposed to more risk but also has

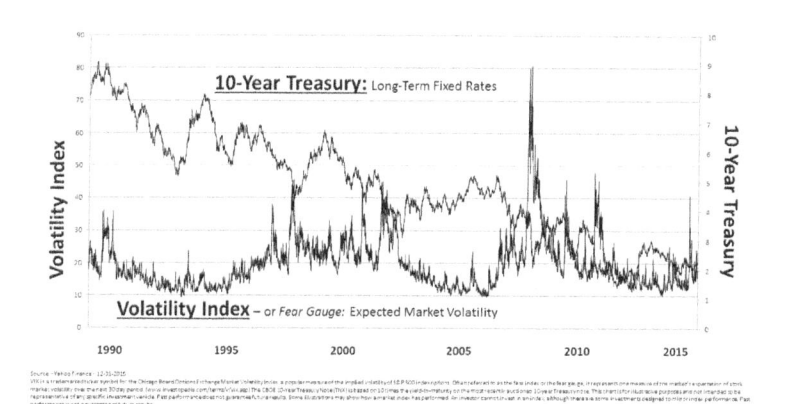

The VIX, or volatility index, of the market represents expected market volatility. When the VIX Drops, economic experts expect less volatility. When the VIX rises, more volatility is expected.

1. VIX is a trademarked ticker symbol for the Chicago Board Options Exchange (CBOE) Market Volatility Index, a popular measure of the implied volatility of S&P 500 index options. Often referred to as the fear index or the fear gauge, it represents one measure of the market's expectation of stock market volatility over the next 30 day period. (wikipedia.com)
2. The CBOE 10-Year Treasury note (TNX) is based on 10 times the yield-to-maturity on the most recently auctioned 10-year Treasury note.

the potential for more reward. Because the market is subject to change, you can't really be sure what the value of your investments will be worth in the future. You can't really *rely* on it at all. For this reason, we refer to it as Hope So Money. This doesn't mean you shouldn't have some money invested in the market, but it would be dangerous to assume you can know what it will be worth in the future.

Hope So Money is an important element of a retirement plan, especially in the early stages of planning when you can trade volatility for potential returns, and when a longer investment timeframe is available to you. In the long run, time can smooth out the ups and downs of money exposed to the market. Working with a professional and leveraging a long-term investment strategy has the potential to create rewarding returns from Hope So Money.

Know So Money, on the other hand, is safer when compared to Hope So Money. Know So Money is made up of dependable, low-risk or no-risk money, and investments that you can count on. Social Security is one of the most common forms of Know So Money. Income you draw or will draw from Social Security is guaranteed. You have paid into Social Security your entire career, and you can rely on that money during your retirement. Unlike the market, rates of growth for Know So Money are dependent on 10-year treasury rates. The 10-year treasury, or TNX, is commonly considered to represent a very secure and safe place for your money, hence Know So Money. The 10-year treasury drives key rates for things such as mortgage rates or CD rates. Know So Money may not be as exciting as Hope So Money, but it is safer. You can safely be fairly sure you will have it in the future.

Knowing the difference between Hope So and Know So Money is an important step towards a successful retirement plan. People who are 55 or older and who are looking ahead to retirement should be relying on more Know So Money than Hope So Money.

Ideally, the rates of return on Hope So and Know So Money would have an overlapping area that provided an acceptable rate of risk for both types of money. In the early 1990s, interest rates were high and market volatility was low. At that time, you could invest in either Hope So or Know So Money options because the rates of return were similar from both Know So and Hope So investments, and you were likely to be fairly successful with a wide range of investment options. At that time, you could expose yourself to an acceptable amount of risk or an acceptable fixed rate. Basically, it was difficult to make a mistake during that time period. Today, you don't have those options. Market volatility is at all-time highs while interest rates are at all-time lows. They are so far apart from each other that it is hard to know what to do with your money.

Yesterday's investment rules may not work today. Not only could they hamper achieving your goals, they may actually harm your financial situation. We are currently in a period when the rates for Know So Money options are at historic lows, and the volatility of Hope So Money is higher than ever. There is no overlapping acceptable rate, making both options less than ideal. *Because of this uncertain financial landscape, wise investment strategies are more important now than ever.*

This unique situation requires fresh ideas and investment tools that haven't been relied on in the past. Investing the way your parents did will not pay off. The majority of investment ideas used by financial professionals in the 1990s aren't applicable to today's markets. That kind of investing will likely get you in trouble and compromise your retirement. Today, you need a better PLAN.

HOW MUCH RISK ARE YOU EXPOSED TO?

Many investors don't know how much risk they are exposed to. It is helpful to organize your assets so you can have a clear understanding of how much of your money is at risk and how much is in safer holdings. This process starts with listing all your assets. Let's take a look at the two kinds of money:

Hope So Money is, as the name indicates, money that you *hope* will be there when you need it. Hope So Money represents what you would like to get out of your investments. Examples of Hope So Money include:
- Stock market funds, including index funds
- Mutual funds
- Variable annuities
- Real estate investment trusts (REITs)

Know So Money is money that you know you can count on. It is safer money that isn't exposed to the level of volatility as the asset types noted above. You can more confidently count on having this money when you need it. Examples of Know So Money are:
- Government backed bonds
- Savings and checking accounts
- Fixed indexed annuities
- Certificates of deposit (CDs)
- Treasuries
- Money market accounts

> » *Jack had a modest brokerage account that he added to when he could. When he changed jobs a couple years ago, at age 58, Jack transferred his 401(k) assets into an IRA. Just a few years from retirement, he is now beginning to realize that nearly every dollar he has saved for retirement is subject to market risk.*

Intuitively, he knows that the time has come to shift some assets to an alternative that is safer, but how much is the right amount?

THE RULE OF 100

Determining the amount of risk that is right for you is dependent on a number of variables. You need to feel comfortable with where and how you are investing your money, and your financial professional is obligated to help you make decisions that put your money in places that fit your risk criteria.

Your retirement needs to first accommodate your day-to-day income needs. How much money do you need to maintain your lifestyle? When do you need it?

Managing your risk by having a balance of Hope So Money vs. Know So Money is a good start that will put you ahead of the curve. But how much Know So Money is enough to secure your income needs during retirement, and how much Hope So Money is enough to allow you to continue to benefit from an improving market?

In short, how do you begin to know how much risk you should be exposed to?

While there is no single approach to investment risk determination advice that is universally applicable to everyone, there are some helpful guidelines. One of the most useful is called *The Rule of 100*. The Rule of 100 is a general rule that helps shape asset diversification* for the average investor. The rule states that the

---

* *Asset Diversification disclosure – Diversification and asset allocation does not assure of guarantee better performance and cannot eliminate the risk of investment loss. Before investing, you should carefully read the applicable volatility disclosure for each of the underlying funds, which can be found in the current prospectus.*

number 100 minus an investor's age equals the amount of assets they should have exposed to risk.

The Rule of 100: 100 - (your age) = the percentage of your assets that should be exposed to risk (Hope So Money)

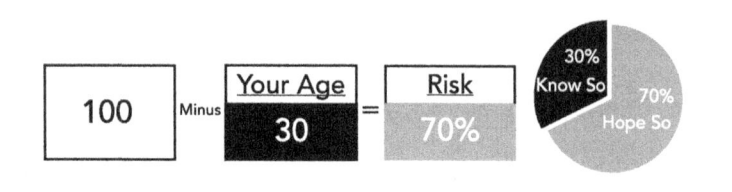

100	Minus	Your Age **30**	=	Risk **70%**

30% Know So
70% Hope So

For example, if you are a 30-year-old investor, the Rule of 100 would indicate that you should be focusing on investing primarily in the market and taking on a substantial amount of risk in your portfolio. The Rule of 100 suggests that 70 percent of your investments should be exposed to risk.

100 - (30 years of age) = 70 percent

Now, not every 30-year-old should have exactly 70 percent of their assets in mutual funds and stocks. The Rule of 100 is based on your chronological age, not your "financial age," which could vary based on your investment experience, your aversion or acceptance of risk and other factors. While this rule isn't an ironclad solution to anyone's finances, it's a pretty good place to start. Once you've taken the time to look at your assets with a professional to determine your risk exposure, you can use the Rule of 100 to make changes that put you in a more stable investment position—one that reflects your comfort level.

Perhaps when you were age 30 and starting your career, like in the example above, it made sense to have 70 percent of your money in the market: you had time on your side. You had plenty of time to save more money, work more and recover from a downturn in the market. Retirement was ages away, and your earning power was increasing. And indeed, younger investors should take on more risk for exactly those reasons. The potential reward of long-term involvement in the market outweighs the risk of investing when you are young.

Risk tolerance generally reduces as you get older, however. If you are 40 years old and lose 30 percent of your portfolio in a market downturn this year, you have 20 or 30 years to recover it. If you are 68 years old, you have five to 10 years (or less) to make the same recovery. That new circumstance changes your whole retirement perspective. At age 68, it's likely that you simply aren't as interested in suffering through a tough stock market. There is less time to recover from downturns, and the stakes are higher. The money you have saved is money you will soon need to provide you with income, or is money that you already need to meet your income demands.

Much of the flexibility that comes with investing earlier in life is related to *compounding*. Compounded earnings can be incredibly powerful over time. The longer your money has time to compound, the greater your wealth will be. This is what most people talk about when they refer to putting their money to work. This is also why the Rule of 100 favors risk for the young. If you start investing when you are young, you can invest smaller amounts of money in a more aggressive fashion because you have the potential to make a profit in a rising market and you can harness the power of compounding earnings. When you are 40, 50 or 60 years old, that potential becomes less and less and you are forced to have more money at lower amounts of risk to realize the same returns. **It basically becomes more expensive to prudently invest the older you get.**

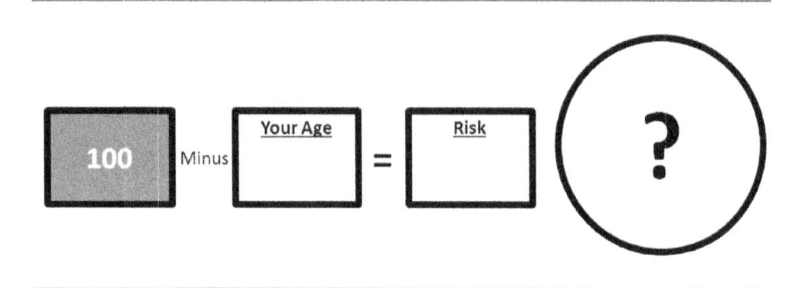

```
[ 100 ] Minus [ Your Age ] = [ Risk ]  ( ? )
```

Everyone has their own level of comfort. Your Rule of 100 results will be based on your values and attitudes as well as your comfort with risk.

The Rule of 100 can apply to overarching financial management and to specific investment products that you own as well. Take the 401(k) for example. Many people have them, but not many people understand how their money is allocated within their 401(k). An employer may have someone who comes in once a year and explains the models and options that employees can choose from, but that's as much guidance as most 401(k) holders get. Many 401(k) options include target date funds that change their risk exposure over time, essentially following a form of the Rule of 100. Selecting one of these options can often be a good move for employees because they shift your risk as you age, securing more Know So Money when you need it.

A financial professional can look at your assets with you and discuss alternatives to optimize your balance between Know So and Hope So Money.

CHAPTER 1 TAKE-AWAY //

- You have to understand what you want your money to do for you before you can figure out where to put it and how and when to take it out.
- Find a fiduciary based financial professional that is able to put all the working parts of your retirement together in a comprehensive guide to ensure your goals are clearly aligned with your customized plan—one that allows you to live the retirement you want with peace of mind.

2
TRUE DIVERSIFICATION

"What we usually consider as impossible are simply engineering problems ... there's no law of physics preventing them."
— Michio Kaku

The average investor needs to accumulate assets to create a retirement plan that provides income during retirement and also allows for legacy planning. To accomplish this, they need to balance the amount of risk to which they are exposed. Risk is required because, while Know So Money is safer, more reliable and more dependable, it doesn't grow very fast, if at all. Today's historically low interest rates barely break even with current inflation. Hope So Money, while less dependable, has more potential for growth. Hope So Money can eventually become Know So Money once you move it to an investment with lower risk. Everyone's risk diversification will be different depending on their goals, age and their existing assets.

So how do you decide how much risk your assets should be exposed to? Where do you begin?

Over the course of your lifetime, it is likely that you have acquired a variety of assets. Assets can range from money that you have in a savings account or a 401(k), to a pension or an IRA. You have earned money and have made financial decisions based on the best information you had at the time. When viewed as a whole, however, you might not have an overall strategy for the management of your assets. As we have seen, it's more important than ever to know which of your assets are at risk. High market volatility and low treasury rates make for challenging financial topography. Navigating this financial landscape starts with true diversification and strategic asset management that takes into account your specific needs and options.

The following story shows what you have to gain by taking the time to get your portfolio diversified in a way that's appropriate for someone entering into retirement.

> *» Trudy was a widow in her early 60s and she needed some help with her asset allocation in preparation for retirement. Her husband had passed away a few years prior, and he handled all their investing. Now that he was gone, she was suddenly responsible for $1 million in stocks and funds, and she knew nothing about what she had or what to do with them.*
>
> *Early in 2013, Trudy decided it was time to talk to someone who specialized in helping people plan for retirement. She came in to see an investment advisor, and when he looked at her portfolio, he told her, "Congratulations, your husband did very well. If we get you set up in an efficient distribution*

plan, you can retire and not have to worry ever again about your money."

Well this was wonderful news; however, Trudy still had to make what felt like a tough decision. The stocks her husband had chosen were not at all diversified. Trudy's portfolio was currently invested in only two things: one half of her money was in a Chinese stock, and the other half was in oil and gas.

Oil and gas up to that point had been the hottest thing in the market, and it had earned her fantastic returns, however, she wasn't diversified properly for someone entering retirement.

Now, her financial professional did not own a crystal ball. He had no idea that gas and oil prices were about to plummet, but he did know how to achieve the true diversification necessary for someone in Trudy's situation. He talked her though why she had to let go of some of these fantastic things in order to prepare for retirement.

"You have enough money," he said, "But only if you don't lose it. In other words, you've made it, and there's no need to take on any extra risk."

Trudy agreed. The professional showed her how to take a portion of her portfolio to set up a secure income and growth plan, using a blend of Know So and tactical managed money investments. She had to let some of her gas and oil stocks go. Unbelievably, this was just one month prior to when those stocks tanked. Looking back at her original portfolio, had Trudy NOT gotten the advice she did and changed her asset allocation, her portfolio would have dropped by over 50 percent, and her $1 million nest egg would have been reduced to $480,000.

Instead, Trudy is happily retired with a balanced portfolio and enjoying an income that she can't outlive.

PULLING BACK THE CURTAIN ON MANAGED FUNDS

Regardless of whether you are managing your funds yourself or leaving it in the hands of a broker, it's crucial to the stability of your retirement to do a thorough inventory and understand the kinds of funds that you are invested in. Trudy's story is just one example of improper diversification, but more commonly what we see are investors who leave their accumulation years under the false assumption that because they have a portfolio labeled as "conservative" or "moderate" in terms of risk, they are properly diversified. Mutual funds or 60/40 portfolios are often pitched as a way to diversify a portfolio, and marketing material and propaganda might have you believe that large firms are doing everything they can to make sure you are properly diversified. Problem is, there's a big difference between the diversification you need during your working years and what you need as someone entering retirement.

There are two points here that need to be made:
1. Working with a broker does not necessarily mean that your fund is being managed in a way that can protect you from loss.
2. True diversification is about much more than having a variety of different funds, stocks and bonds.

First, let's define the difference between managed funds and actively managed money. Most people working with a big firm are under the belief that their money is being managed, and that this fund manager has the ability to take care of them, or "get them out" of the fund, when things look like they are going south. Unfortunately, this is not the case.

Fund managers must follow strict investing guidelines. According to the Securities and Exchange Commission (SEC), any mutual fund with a name suggesting that it focuses on a particular type of investment is required *"to invest at least 80 percent* *of its assets in the type of investment suggested by its name."** So, for example, if you were invested in a technology fund in early 2000, and the tech stocks started to drop, your portfolio probably lost a significant amount. You might have looked at your statements with alarm and wondered, "*Why isn't my broker doing anything?*"

The answer: there wasn't anything he could do. **Even if the fund manager read all the signs and knew that devastation was on its way, he or she is not able to go to a safe place.**

So what are your other options?

Enter *tactical managed money*. **There are independent, third-party money managers who ACTIVELY manage your money and they have full rights to go to cash positions overnight based on data, market conditions, the political environment, or whatever else might be going on in the macro-economy of our world.** These are what we call "actively managed strategies" and this is the kind of tactical money management that can work in your favor during your distribution years. When you are being actively managed, you might still be invested in technology funds, but instead of having to follow the objectives of a mutual fund prospectus, your fund managers have more control and ability to move in and out of the market to follow *your* preferences for risk tolerance.

TRUE DIVERSIFICATION:
GETTING IN ON THE BEST WITHOUT THE WORST
Having a diversified portfolio means that no single investment is relied on as the best answer or the only solution, but rather a blended investment strategy is employed.

Your strategy will be designed specifically for you, based on your current asset base, risk tolerance and retirement goals. When you work with a distribution specialist, your strategy will contain

---

* *https://www.sec.gov/rules/final/ic-24828.htm*

two important ingredients: an element of Know So Money to secure your income, and tactical managed money options for your growth needs.

Tactical money management adheres to proper diversification and risk appropriate portfolio selections across market cycles. The objectives of tactical money are the same any investor has when entering the market: growth. However, these investments are structured differently.

For example, instead of putting X amount of money in stocks and X amount of bonds and saying, "thank you, have a nice day," tactical investors seek to protect you from losses bigger than 5 or 10 percent. Once way they do that is by using inverse market options. These inverse options are able to earn returns when other market investments go down, so you are given a layer of protective returns that cushion your fall against large drops.

Another strategy is to use computer algorithms generated by proprietary strategies that track the stock market on a daily basis in order to detect signs of a potential coming disaster, and if so, move the money off to the side—in cash. This is different from panicking once you start to lose money, then taking it out of a fund once it hits near bottom, and keeping it in cash while the fund recovers. Tactical money managers don't sit around a table deciding when to get out of the market, but rather they rely on tested means and algorithms that let them know when it's time to go to a safer position.

You might say that a broker looks at the market in terms of keeping you IN so you don't miss the best days, while active money managers look at the market in terms of getting you OUT so you aren't destroyed on the worst days.

Statistics have shown that by getting out during the worst moments such as during 2002 or from 2007 to 2008, investors are able to achieve healthier portfolios. By not taking these huge loses, the ability to compound your money is not lost, and so you are able to maintain the growth you need to thrive during the 20 to 30 years that can make up a retirement.

So, how diversified is your portfolio? Even if you feel that you have plenty of money in your 401(k) or IRA, not knowing how much *risk* those investments are exposed to can cause you major financial suffering. One of the easiest ways to understand your current allocation is to use a color system for your money.

THE COLOR OF MONEY

The colors red, green and yellow can be used to identify the different levels of risk your investments are exposed to. Each color has unique benefits and features.

- Green Money is known as safe money. While no investment is completely without risk, these investments employ safer strategies for income protection during retirement. Green Money is money that you know you can count on. It is safer money that isn't exposed to the level of volatility as the asset types noted below. You can more confidently count on having this money when you need it.
- Red Money is known as risk money. These investments are exposed to the risk and fluctuation of the stock market, but they provide growth opportunities for your money. Red Money represents what you would like to get out of your investments.
- Yellow Money is actively managed money. It is still invested in Red Money, but you have more control and the ability to move depending on the environment. We will go into more depth about tactical money management in Chapter 7.

The fact of the matter is that a lot of people don't know their level of exposure to risk. Visually organizing your assets is an important and powerful way to get a clear picture of what kind of money you

Green Money	Red Money	Yellow Money
"Green Money" is safer.	"Red Money" is at risk.	"Yellow Money" is actively managed money.
This is money that offers a minimum guarantee but it may pose risks other than market risk.	This is money that can go up or down in value. It may pose risk if it is not properly managed to serve a specific purpose in a comprehensive plan.	Yellow Money is still invested in Red Money but there is more control over the investment.

have, where it is and how you can best use it in the future. This process is as simple as listing your assets and assigning them a color. Work with your financial professional to create a comprehensive inventory of your assets to understand what you are working with before making any decisions. This may be the first time you have ever sat down and sorted out all of your assets, allowing you to see how much money you have at risk in the market. A lot of people are surprised to find how much of their portfolio is actually in Red Money investments. Investors in a "conservative" portfolio are usually not comfortable with losing more than 10 percent of their money, even if they aren't nearing retirement, yet this is what can happen without true diversification. **By the very label used to describe asset allocation, it's easy to be misled about your actual exposure to risk.** Using the Color of Money concept is one way to visualize your risk so you can start getting your assets organized in a way that better prepares you for the challenges of the distribution years.

PRE-SELECT YOUR RISK: WHAT ARE YOU COMFORTABLE WITH?

The way you organize your assets depends on your goals and your level of comfort with risk. Whatever you determine the appropriate amount of risk for you to be, you will need to organize your portfolio to reflect your goals. The next step is to know the right amount and ratio of Green and Red Money for you at your stage of retirement planning.

Investing heavily in Red Money and gambling ALL of your assets on the market is incredibly risky no matter where you fall within the Rule of 100. Money in the market can't be depended on to generate income, and a plan that leans too heavily on Red Money can easily fail, especially when investment decisions are influenced by emotional reactions to market downturns and recoveries. Not only is this an unwise plan, it can be incredibly stressful to an investor who is gambling everything on stocks and mutual funds.

But a plan that uses too much Green Money avoids all volatility and can also fail. Why? Investing all of your money in Certificates of Deposit (CDs), savings accounts, money markets and other low return accounts may provide interest and income, but that likely won't be enough to keep pace with inflation. If you focus exclusively on income from Green Money and avoid owning any stocks or mutual funds in your portfolio, you won't be able to leverage the potential for long-term growth your portfolio needs to stay healthy and productive.

Wouldn't it be nice if you could order the amount of risk you were comfortable with the same way you select dinner items from a menu? When you work with an independent investment advisor, you have the option to choose from a veritable buffet of investments because diversification is about more than just having a lot of eggs in your basket. It's about having investments that behave differently from one another depending on the conditions in the environment.

One way to determine the behavior of your current investment allocation is to run helpful reports that can take a look under the hood of the investment, so to speak, so you can identify inefficiencies, redundancies and dangers likely to bog down your lifestyle.

After a financial professional has gathered all the data about your different holdings, he or she can use sophisticated computer software to analyze your portfolio's performance. There are many different kinds of reports that a professional can run for you to determine fund performance and fee structure. Other reports are used to help analyze specific products or benefits. The following list is designed to give you an idea of what's available:

- **Morningstar Report**: Morningstar is a third-party research company that collects all the information on your portfolio and does an unbiased breakdown of the risk involved, the fees and other areas of information on your investments. Not only does the report look at current returns and fees, but it also looks at how the portfolio might perform in the future. For example, it can look at how much you would stand to lose if a situation like 2008 happened again. The report also takes a hard look at front-load fees on mutual funds that can charge investors anywhere from 5 to 5.75 just to get into the fund. Very few people are aware they are paying these fees. This report can bring it all into the light.
- **Portfolio Stress Report**: This report takes a look at how your portfolio would perform in certain scenarios. What would happen if oil prices went up? What if there was a slowdown in China's economy? What if mortgage interest rates went up? What if gasoline prices go back up over $4 per gallon? You can put your portfolio through this report to test how it performs under these various stressful conditions.
- **The Income Rider Report**: This report is specific to annuities. Income riders are purchased in order to generate an income from an annuity. Income riders can guarantee this income for the rest of your life and even the life of your spouse, which is why this report can be an invaluable tool for anyone looking to get a Know So element into their portfolio. The Income Rider Report runs a test on every participating insurance company out there offering

TRUE DIVERSIFICATION

these income riders to find out which one will give you the best deal for what you need. The report reveals four valuable pieces of information you want to pay specific attention to:

» THE BONUS: In order to attract customers, insurance companies sometimes offer investors a 5, 10 or 20 percent bonus for singing up. This "free money" prize can be hard to ignore, but you have to keep reading and look at the bigger picture. **When you purchase an income rider, you create a secondary account that CANNOT be accessed as one lump sum.** The money in this account can only be accessed as your monthly income payment, which is why you want to look *past* the delicious bonus number and *keep reading*.

» THE ROLL UP: This number tells you the rate the money in that secondary income account will grow. For example, if your roll up is 5 percent, then the amount in the income rider account will grow by 5 percent annually.

» THE GROWTH: There are two ways the growth of your account can be calculated: either simple or compound. **Simple** means the growth is tacked onto the principle. So, for example, if you put $200,000 in using our example of a 5 percent roll up, then every year you would get another 5 percent or $10,000 added to your account. **Compound** means the roll up amount is calculated based on the new total. For example, during year two, you would get 5 percent of $210,000, which is another $10,500 instead of just another $10,000. Over time, compounding is a powerful tool.

» THE PAYOUT: This is the percentage amount used to calculate your actual income. You want to pay very close attention to this number, because many people are tricked by those big bonuses, only to realize they are getting less income from their money. Remember: the money in the secondary account created by the income rider cannot be accessed as a lump sum. For example, if you have $230,000 in your income account thanks to the bonus, but your payout is only 4 percent, then your income will be $9,200 annually. Now imagine you resisted the bonus money and instead put your $200,000 where it earned a 6 percent payout; now your income is $12,000 annually. If this income is guaranteed FOR LIFE, then you will be getting that $12,000 whether you live to be 85 or 105. Imagine that this is a joint account for both you and your spouse, and you'll see how that annual difference of $2,800 would add up to an additional $56,000 over a 20-year retirement. If one of you lives another 10 years, then that's another $28,000 on top of that. Makes the bonus amount look pretty paltry, doesn't it?

- **The Social Security Maximization Report**: This report is not based on an investment product, but rather it's a service offered by investment advisors who care about the overall well-being of their clients. The report generates an individualized understanding of how and when to file for your Social Security so you can optimize this important benefit. Social Security employees can give you information, but they are prevented from providing actual advice and recommendations about how you can maximize your individual situation. This is because they aren't trained in the area of distribution planning, and there are many factors that affect how and when you should file for your benefit. Taxes are also a big part of the picture, which is why running the report is only the first step, as we will discuss later in Chapter 4.

THE NUMBERS DON'T LIE

During your distribution years, it's all about whether or not your income needs are met. Is your current advisor talking to you about your income needs? Are they as concerned as you are about where this money is coming from, how long it will last and how it affects all the other parts of your plan? Risk tolerance is about more than just earning returns during retirement, it's about your portfolio's ability to consistently generate the amount of income you need.

- How much you are getting?
- Where you are pulling that money from?
- Is it guaranteed to last as long as you live?

A professional may encourage you to be more aggressive with your investment strategy by taking on more risk in order to give you the potential of earning a greater return. If your income needs can be met without taking that risk, then wouldn't you want to know about the safer option?

When determining the position of your assets, it's vital to your distribution plan that you know how you are going to structure your income flow. This entails knowing how much you need, what your income gap is, and then identifying which assets will fill that need both now and in the future. How much do you need? The answer to this question dictates how you determine your risk tolerance. If the numbers say that you need to be more aggressive with your investing, or that you need to modify your lifestyle, it becomes a choice you need to make.

WHO IS LOOKING OUT FOR YOUR BEST INTEREST?

Organizing your assets, understanding the color of your money, and creating an income and accumulation plan for retirement can quickly become an overwhelming task. The fact of the matter is that financial professionals build their careers around understanding the different variables affecting retirement financing. They can help you assess the risk inside your current portfolio allocations by running different reports in order to determine which allocations will better meet your goals. Other reports such as the Income Rider Report can help you determine what companies offer the best of a certain type of investment product.

The ability to shop around for investments that specifically fit your needs speaks again to the care you must use when choosing your financial professional. Large brokerage firms are often aligned with certain mutual fund and insurance companies, so you aren't able to take advantage of the information brought to light by these reports, because they can only offer you the products sold under their umbrella. When you find a financial professional who is independent, their firm is not aligned with any one company. Their loyalty is to YOU, the client, which means they can go out and choose from underneath a veritable field of umbrellas to find the investment that best serves you.

Working with a Registered Investment Advisor means working with a professional who is legally obligated to help you make financial decisions that are in your best interest and fall within your comfort zone. Taking steps toward creating a retirement plan is nothing to take lightly. By leveraging tax strategies, properly organizing your assets, and accumulating helpful financial products that help you meet your income and accumulation needs, you are more likely to meet your goals. You might have a million dollars socked away in a savings account, but your neighbor, who has $300,000 in a diverse investment portfolio that is tailored to their needs, may end up enjoying a better retirement lifestyle. Why?

They had more than a good work ethic and a penchant for saving. They had a strategic approach to retirement asset allocation.

CHAPTER 2 TAKE-AWAY //
- True diversification is needed to achieve the risk necessary for a proper retirement investment plan.
- Utilize actively managed strategies in retirement that aim to drive more consistent market gains while limiting market losses.
- Make sure your financial professional has the ability to run comparison reports across the insurance industry finding the companies that provides you the best products at that time—not what provides them the highest commission.

3
INCOME: GETTING IT TOGETHER

"Manufacturing is more than just putting parts together. It's coming up with ideas, testing principles and perfecting the engineering, as well as the final assembly."
– James Dyson

Structuring assets to create an income-generating retirement requires a different approach than earning income via the workforce. Saving money for retirement, which is what you have spent your life doing, and getting it all together to supply a retirement income are two different things. Both are important. Add the complexities of taxes, required minimum distributions (RMDs) from IRAs and legacy planning, and you can begin to see why happy endings require more than hope. They need the strategies behind a well-engineered plan.

Take a moment to think about your income goals:
- What is your lifestyle today?
- Would you like to maintain it into retirement?
- Are you meeting your needs?
- Are you happy with your lifestyle?
- What do you really *need* to live on when you retire?

Some people will have the luxury of maintaining or improving their lifestyle, while others may have to make decisions about what they need versus what they want during their retirement.

HOW MUCH MONEY DO YOU NEED?

An important aspect of your financial plan is the evaluation of your income needs. Finding the most efficient and beneficial way to address them will have impacts on your lifestyle, your asset accumulation and your legacy planning after you retire. When you have identified your income need, you will know how much to structure for income and how much to be set aside for accumulation.

Every financial strategy for retirement needs first to accommodate the day-to-day need for income. The moment your working income ceases and you start living off the money you've set aside for retirement is referred to as the **retirement cliff**. When you begin drawing income from your retirement assets, you have entered the distribution phase of your financial plan. *The distribution phase of your retirement plan* is when you reach the point of relying on your assets for income.

This is where your Green Money comes into play: the safer, more reliable assets that you have accumulated that are designed to provide you with a steady income. On day one of your retirement, you will need a steady and reliable supply of income from your Green Money. While this amount will be different for everyone, the general rule of thumb is that a retiree will require 70 to 80 percent of their pre-retirement income to maintain their lifestyle. Once you know what that number is, the key becomes matching your income need with the correct investment strategies, options and tools to satisfy that need.

WHAT IS YOUR GAP?

The moment that you stop working and start living off the money that you've set aside for retirement can be referred to as the **Retirement Cliff**. You've worked and earned money your whole life, but the day that you retire, that income comes to an end. That's the day that you have to have other assets that fill the gap. Social Security will fill in some, but you need to come up with something else. After you have calculated your Social Security benefit and have selected the year and month that will maximize your lifetime benefits, it's time to look at your other retirement assets, incomes and options that will reduce or eliminate the drop-off of the Retirement Cliff. You may have a pension, an IRA or Roth IRA, dividends from stock holdings, money from the sale of real estate, rental property, or other sources of income. What other sources of reliable income do you have?

If your monthly Social Security check and your other supplemental income leaves a shortfall in your *desired* income, how are you going to fix it? This shortfall is called the **Income Gap** and it needs to be filled in order to maintain your lifestyle into retirement. If you have a known income gap that you need to fill, you want to know how to fill that income gap with the fewest dollars possible. You basically want to buy that income gap for the least amount of money possible. You don't want it to cost you too much, because you want to get the most out of your other assets, including planning for your future and planning for your legacy.

There are two ways of filling the income gap:

1. You can fill your income gap by using "conservative" stock market investments that are Red Money Hope So investments.
2. You can fill your gap by locking in your income using Green Money Know So investments.

Ideally, you want to see if you can get as much of your income guaranteed as possible. Your risk tolerance is an important indicator of what kinds of investments you should consider, but if the returns from those investments don't meet your retirement goals, your income needs will likely not be met. For example, if the level of risk you are comfortable with manages your investments at a 4 percent return and you need to realize an 8 percent return, your income needs aren't going to be met. If taking more risk isn't an option that you are comfortable with, then the discussion will turn to how you can earn more money or spend less in order to align your needs with your resources more closely.

WHEN DO YOU NEED YOUR MONEY?

How long does your retirement income need to last? While no one knows for sure how long they will live, we can use various tools to help us determine the timing of income gaps. Some people find that their income gap increases as they get older; other people find that because of their RMDs, their income gap decreases. As part of a comprehensive plan, your financial professional should take a look at **Future Income Planning** and how that future income is structured.

The issue of Future Income Planning is of particular importance if you have an IRA. With traditional IRAs, the Federal government requires that you begin taking out an income from these accounts whether you need the money or not. These Required Minimum Distributions, also known as RMDs, are mandated once a retiree hits the magic birthday of 70 ½. The penalties for ignoring this rule and not taking the income are steep, so even if you don't need to use the money, *you will want to have a plan in place that can help you best use the rules to your advantage.* Not having a plan for your RMD income can result in a bad surprise on your tax bill come April. In order to avoid jumping into a higher tax bracket, plan ahead for your RMDs, or Uncle Sam will happily reap the rewards of this inefficiency.

Other future concerns include appropriate income adjustments for inflation, the concern over increased health care costs and the expense of long-term care. The U.S. Department of Health and Human Services reports that 70 percent of people turning age 65 can expect to use some form of long-term care during their lives.* Traditional long-term care insurance has gotten difficult to qualify for and very expensive, plus if you never use this type of insurance, then all the money paid into the policy is lost. There are better ways to solve this problem that can leverage your money for your spouse and loved ones while still filling your income gap. When designing a 360-degree plan, these future issues are brought up and alternative solutions are offered. Asset-based policies do exist that can provide far more attractive benefits than traditional long-term care insurance policies. Ask your financial professional what options might best fit your situation.

So how do you figure out how much you need and when you need it? When you take health care costs, potential emergencies, plans for moving or traveling, and other retirement expenses into account, you can really give your calculator a workout. You want to maximize retirement benefits to meet your lifetime income needs. An investment advisor can help you answer those questions by working with you to customize an income plan.

As we determined earlier in Chapter 1, the most important thing you need to do as you create an income plan is to take

---

* *http://longtermcare.gov/the-basics/who-needs-care/*

care to avoid too much exposure to risk. You can start by meeting with an investment advisor to organize your assets. Get your Green Money and Red Money in order and balanced to meet your needs. If the market goes down 18 percent this afternoon, you don't want that to come out of what you're relying on for next year's income.

Hot on the heels of securing your Green Money, it's time to structure those Green Money assets so they can generate income for you. Ultimately, you have to take care of your monthly income needs to pay the bills. The Big Kahuna of Green Money is your Social Security benefit.

CHAPTER 3 TAKE-AWAY //

- If you don't plan for your income needs during retirement, problems such as market loss, taxes, inflation and long-term care costs can sneak up on you, and once they do, it may be too late to solve them.

4
OPTIMIZING SOCIAL SECURITY

"There are hundreds of miracles within a single machine. Americans calmly explain these with mathematical formulas."
— Warren Eyster

Most Americans know they can rely on Social Security as part of their retirement income, but did you know that there are 2,728 different mathematical formulas that can affect the amount of your overall lifetime income?* Social Security is a benefit you have paid into your entire working career, and it is designed to pay you a lifetime income. Claiming your benefit at the wrong time can

---

* *www.forbes.com/sites/kotlikoff/2012/07/03/44-social-security-secrets-allbaby-boomers-and-millions-of-current-recipients-need-to-know/*

potentially cost you thousands of dollars when you consider the number of years your benefit might be paying you. For a married couple aged 62 today, there is a 95 percent chance that at least one of you will live to the age of 75, and a 65 percent that chance one of you will live another ten years past that, to age 85.* Unfortunately, many people are ill-advised by their broker, friend or a well-meaning neighbor to file for Social Security early, at age 62. Waiting to file means you will have a Green Money investment that is growing or rolling up by a guaranteed 8 percent annually in delayed retirement credits.**

When is the best time to file for you? That all depends on a number of factors, but one thing is true for everyone: it makes sense to engineer a strategy that can help you optimize this benefit so you can get the most out of it.

TAX STRATEGY AND YOUR SOCIAL SECURITY BENEFIT

With all things being equal, the more income you can get from your Social Security dollars, the fewer dollars you need from your other investments. A "strategy" when referring to this Green Money benefit is used to denote a set of Social Security claiming ages, techniques and tax consideration, rather than a given investment strategy. Perhaps the most intriguing piece of the Social Security puzzle is how your benefit will be taxed. **Social Security income falls under the category we call tax-preferred income.** This means it is not taxed the same way as your other retirement income.

---

* *The SOCIAL SECURITY CLAIMING GUIDE, Center for Financial Literacy at Boston College, 2009*

** *www.socialsecurity.gov/retire2/1943.htm*

What percentage of your qualified account distributions such as your IRA, RMDs and 401(k) are subject to taxes? The answer: 100 percent.

What percent of your Social Security income is subject to taxes? The answer: 0 to 85 percent, depending on your other income sources and how you engineer your strategy.

Consider the following story that shows you how working with an investment advisor who is knowledgeable about Social Security can help you earn more money by saving money on your tax obligations during retirement:

> *» Joe is a hardworking individual who likes to follow the rules, whereas his wife, Sue, likes to test things and ask questions. Together, they make a pretty good team. At age 62, they are both thinking about retiring in three years' time. They know they have an income need of $80,000 of income a year and have two expected sources of income: their Social Security benefits, and the money in their IRA. What they don't know is how best to use these two assets in order to get the income amount they need.*
>
> *To get some advice, Joe asks his broker when they should claim their Social Security benefit. Without asking Joe any questions about his plans, the broker tells them to file now, at age 62.*
>
> *"Why not file?" the broker explains. "You're entitled to it. You might as well get it while you can."*
>
> *Well that made sense to Joe, but when he tells his wife what the broker suggested, she makes a face.*
>
> *"He doesn't know anything about Social Security," she says. "I think we need to get a second opinion."*
>
> *"Okay," says, Joe. "Should I call the Social Security Administration?"*

"Absolutely not," says Sue. *"They can't tell you a darn thing either. All they do is help you fill out the paperwork."*

Sue finds them an investment advisor who sits down with them and looks at the bigger picture of their retirement in terms of their income needs for the next 30 years. He also asks them questions about their plans, and when he learns that Joe and Sue plan to work until age 65, he explains that until you hit Full Retirement Age (FRA), Social Security will reduce your benefit by $1 for every $2 earned above the annual limit. The annual limit for 2016 is only $15,702.* *Joe at his current job earns much more than that. If he waits to claim his benefit until after he turns 66 (FRA,) then he can work as much as he wants to without any penalty to his Social Security income. Furthermore, by not claiming their benefit too early, they can let it grow requiring less of their IRA money as income, thus potentially lowering their future taxes.*

The advisor then discusses the importance of the taxation of their Social Security income. For example, Joe and Sue were previously advised to file "early" at age 62. At that time they expect to receive $30,000 a year from Social Security, and thus withdraw $50,000 a year from their IRA money. Their estimated total taxable income, based on the provisional income formula, would be $73,850.

As an alternate strategy, their new investment advisor runs them a Social Security Maximization Report, and designs a strategy for them that takes a closer look at how their benefit will be taxed. By waiting until age 70, Joe and Sue expect to receive $60,000 a year from Social Security, requiring them to only take out $20,000 a year from their IRA at that time. Because of the tax-preferred status of their Social Security in-

---

* http://www.ssa.gov/retire2/whileworking.htm

come, their total taxable income at age 70 is estimated to only be $31,100. By working together with their new financial professional, Joe and Sue are able to use the rules to their advantage and keep more of their benefit dollars.

Not everyone should delay taking their Social Security, and there are many considerations besides benefit amount and taxation that go into making this decision, but by working with a qualified professional, you can learn how to make the most out of your situation. Here are a few facts about how Social Security income is taxed:

- **For an individual filing a Federal tax return:**
  » If your combined income is less than $25,000, then there is no income tax on your Social Security benefit.
  » If your combined income is between $25,000 and $34,000, you may have to pay income tax on up to 50 percent of your benefits.
  » If your combined income is more than $34,000, then up to 85 percent of your benefits may be taxable.
- **For a couple filing a joint return:**
  » If you and your spouse have a combined income less than $32,000, then there is no income tax on your Social Security benefit.
  » If you and your spouse have a combined income between $32,000 and $44,000, you may have to pay income tax on up to 50 percent of your benefits.

> » If you and your spouse have a combined income of more than $44,000, then up to 85 percent of your benefits may be taxable.*

SOCIAL SECURITY FACTS

There are many aspects of Social Security that are well known and others that aren't. When it comes time for you to cash in on your Social Security benefit, you will have many options and choices. Social Security is a massive government program that manages retirement benefits for millions of people. Experts spend their entire careers understanding and analyzing it. Luckily, you don't have to understand all of the intricacies of Social Security to maximize its advantages. You simply need to know the best way to manage your Social Security benefit. You need to know exactly what to do to get the most from your Social Security benefit and when to do it. Taking the time to create a roadmap for your Social Security strategy will help ensure that you are able to exact your maximum benefit and efficiently coordinate it with the rest of your retirement plan.

Here are some facts that illustrate how Americans currently use Social Security:

- Nearly 90 percent of Americans age 65 and older receive Social Security benefits.**
- Social Security provides about 34 percent of the income of the elderly.**
- Claiming Social Security benefits at the wrong time can reduce your monthly benefit by up to 65 percent.***

---

* *https://www.ssa.gov/policy/docs/issuepapers/ip2015-02.html*
** *https://www.ssa.gov/news/press/factsheets/basicfact-alt.pdf*
*** *https://www.ssa.gov/planners/retire/retirechart.html*

- In 2013, more than a third of workers claimed Social Security benefits as soon they became eligible.*
- In 2016, the average monthly Social Security benefit was $1,341. *The maximum benefit for 2016 was $2,639. The $1,298 monthly benefit reduction between the average and the maximum is applied for life.***

There are many aspects of Social Security that you have no control over. You don't control how much you put into it, and you don't control what it's invested in or how the government manages it. However, you do control when and how you file for benefits. The real question about Social Security that you need to answer is, "When should I start taking Social Security?" While this is the all-important question, there are a couple of key pieces of information you need to track down first.

Before we get into a few calculations and strategies that can make all the difference, let's start by covering the basic information about Social Security which should give you an idea of where you stand. Just as the foundation of a house creates the stable platform for the rest of the framework to rest upon, your Social Security benefit is an important part of your overall retirement plan. The purpose of the information that follows is not to give an exhaustive explanation of how Social Security works, but to give you some tools and questions to start understanding how Social Security affects your retirement and how you can prepare for it.

Let's start with eligibility.

---

* *Trends in Social Security Claiming*, Alicia H Munnell and Anqi Chen, Center for Retirement Research, May 2015. http://crr.bc.edu/wp-content/uploads/2015/05/IB_15-8.pdf

** https://www.ssa.gov/news/press/factsheets/colafacts2016.html

Eligibility. Understanding how and when you are eligible for Social Security benefits will help clarify what to expect when the time comes to claim them.

To receive retirement benefits from Social Security, you must earn eligibility. In almost all cases, Americans born after 1929 must earn 40 quarters of credit to be eligible to draw their Social Security retirement benefit. In 2016, a Social Security credit represents $1,260 earned in a calendar quarter. The number changes as it is indexed each year, but not drastically. In 2015, a credit represented $1,220. Four quarters of credit is the maximum number that can be earned each year. In 2016, an American would have had to earn at least $5,040 to accumulate four credits. In order to qualify for retirement benefits, you must have earned a minimum number of credits. Although 40 is the minimum number of credits required to begin drawing benefits, it is important to know that once you claim your Social Security benefit, you are essentially locked into that base benefit amount forever. Additionally, if you are at least 62 years old, have been married for at least 12 months, and your spouse is currently collecting his or her own retirement benefit, then you can choose to receive Spousal Benefits based on your spouse's work record.

Primary Insurance Amount. Your primary insurance amount (PIA) is the dollar amount your monthly benefit will be when you reach your full retirement age (FRA). In other words, your PIA represents 100 percent of the monthly benefit to which you are entitled. If you opt to take benefits before your FRA, your monthly benefit will be less than your PIA. If you opt to delay taking benefits past your FRA, however, your monthly benefit will be more than your PIA. For example, if you filed at age 62, your monthly benefit would be 75 percent of your PIA. But if you waited to file until you were 70 years old and your FRA was age 66, your benefit would be 132 percent of your PIA. When it comes to filing for Social Security, timing is everything. You can think of your Social Security benefit as a ripening fruit—the goal is to pick the fruit when you can get the most out of it. If you file for benefits too early, you will be locked into receiving a monthly benefit amount less than the full amount to which you are entitled—you will essentially be picking an unripe fruit. On the other hand, the longer you wait to file the more your monthly benefit will increase, but every month you wait is one less check you'll get from the government—you don't want to wait too long and let the fruit become overripe.

Full Retirement Age. Your FRA is an important figure for anyone who is planning to rely on Social Security benefits in their retirement. Depending on when you were born, there is a specific age at which you will attain FRA. Your FRA is dictated by your year of birth and is the age at which you can begin receiving your PIA. Your FRA is important because it is half of the equation used to calculate your Social Security benefit. The other half of the equation is based on when you start taking benefits.

When Social Security was initially set up, the FRA was age 65, and it still is for people born before 1938. But as time has passed, the age for receiving full retirement benefits has increased. If you were born between 1938 and 1960, your full retirement age is somewhere on a sliding scale between 65 and 67. Anyone born in 1960 or later will now have to wait until age 67 for full benefits. Increasing the FRA has helped the government reduce the cost of the Social Security program, which paid out almost $918 billion to beneficiaries in 2016!*

While you can begin collecting retirement benefits as early as age 62, the amount you receive as a monthly benefit will be less than it would be if you wait until you reach or surpass your FRA. It is important to note that if you file for your Social Security benefit before your FRA, ***the reduction to your monthly benefit***

---

* *https://www.ssa.gov/news/press/factsheets/basicfact-alt.pdf*

will remain in place for the rest of your life. You can also delay receiving benefits up to age 70, in which case your benefits will be higher than your PIA for the rest of your life.

- At FRA, 100 percent of PIA is available as a monthly benefit.
- At age 62, your Social Security retirement benefits are available. For each month you take benefits prior to your FRA, however, the monthly amount of your benefit is reduced. ***This reduction stays in place for the rest of your life.***
- At age 70, your monthly benefit reaches its maximum. After you turn age 70, your monthly benefit will no longer increase.

Year of birth	Full Retirement Age
1943-1954	66
1955	66 and 2 months
1956	66 and 4 months
1957	66 and 6 months
1958	66 and 8 months
1959	66 and 10 months
1960 or later	67*

ROLLING UP YOUR SOCIAL SECURITY

Your Social Security income "rolls up" the longer you wait to claim it. Your monthly benefit will continue to increase until you turn 70 years old. Even though Social Security is the foundation of most people's retirement, many Americans feel that they don't have control over how or when they receive their benefits. The truth is that every dollar you increase your Social Security income by means less money you will have to spend from your nest egg

---

* *http://www.ssa.gov/OACT/progdata/nra.html*

to meet your retirement income needs, but many retirees do not take advantage of this fact. For many people, creating their Social Security strategy is the most important decision they can make to positively impact their retirement. *The difference between the best and worst Social Security decision can be tens of thousands of dollars over a lifetime of benefits.*

Deciding NOW or LATER: Following the above logic, it makes sense to wait as long as you can to begin receiving your Social Security benefit. However, the answer isn't always that simple. Not everyone has the option of waiting. Many people need to rely on Social Security on day one of their retirement. Some might need the income. Others might be in poor health and don't feel they will live long enough to make waiting until their FRA worthwhile for themselves or their families. It is also possible, however, that the majority of folks taking an early benefit at age 62 are simply under-informed about Social Security. Perhaps they make this major decision based on rumors and emotion.

File Immediately if You:
- Find your job is unbearable.
- Are willing to sacrifice retirement income.
- Are not healthy and need a reliable source of income.
- Are not concerned about increasing your survivor or dependent benefits.

Consider Delaying Your Benefit if You:
- Want to maximize your retirement income.
- Want to increase survivor benefits for your spouse.
- Are still working and like it.
- Are healthy and willing / able to wait to file.

So if you decide to wait, how long should you wait? Lots of people can put it off for a few years, but not everyone can wait until they are 70 years old. Your individual circumstances may be able to help you determine when you should begin taking Social Security. If you do the math, you will quickly see that between ages 62 and 70, there are 96 months in which you can file for your Social Security benefit. If you take into account those 96 months and the 96 months your spouse could also file for Social Security, and the number of different strategies for structuring your benefit, you can easily end up with more than 20,000 different scenarios. It's safe to say this isn't the kind of math that most people can easily handle. Each month would result in a different benefit amount. The longer you wait, the higher your monthly benefit amount becomes. Each month you wait, however, is one less month that you receive a Social Security check.

The goal is to get the most out of your benefit. That may not always mean waiting until you can get the largest monthly payment. Taking the bigger picture into account, you want to find out how to get the most money out of Social Security over the number of years that you draw from it. Don't underestimate the power of optimizing your benefit: the difference between the BEST and WORST Social Security election can easily be worth thousands of dollars in lifetime benefits. *The difference can be very substantial!*

If you know that every month you wait, your Social Security benefit goes up a little bit, and you also know that every month you wait, you receive one less benefit check, how do you determine where the sweet spot is that maximizes your benefits over your lifetime? Financial professionals have access to software that will calculate the best year and month for you to file for benefits based on your default life expectancy. You can further customize that information by estimating your life expectancy based on your health, habits and family history. If you can then create an income plan (we'll get into this later in the chapter) that helps you wait until the target date for you to file for Social Security, you can optimize your retirement income strategy to get the most out of your Social Security benefit. How can you calculate your life expectancy? Well, you don't know exactly how long you'll live, but you have a better idea than the government does. They rely on averages to make their calculations. **You have much more personal information about your health, lifestyle and family history than they do.** You can use that knowledge to game the system and beat all the other people who are making uninformed decisions by filing early for Social Security.

While you can and should educate yourself about how Social Security works, the reality is you don't need to know a lot of general information about Social Security in order to make choices about your retirement. What you do need to know is exactly **what to do to maximize your benefit.** Because knowing what you need to do has huge impacts on your retirement! For most Americans, Social Security is the foundation of income planning for retirement. Social Security benefits represent about 34 percent of the income of the elderly.* For many people, it can represent the largest portion of their retirement income. Not treating your Social Security benefit as an asset and investment tool can lead to sub-optimization of your largest source of retirement income.

Let's take a look at an example that shows the impact of working with a financial professional to optimize Social Security benefits:

> » *Dennis and Lavone Conner are a typical American couple who have worked their whole lives and saved when they could. Dennis is 60 years old, and Lavone is 56 years old. They sat down with a financial professional who logged onto the Social Security website to look up their PIAs. Dennis's PIA is $1,900 and Lavone's is $900.*

---

* *http://www.socialsecurity.gov/pressoffice/basicfact.htm*

If the Conners cash in at age 62 and begin taking retirement benefits from Social Security, they will receive an estimated $568,600 in lifetime benefits. That may seem like a lot, but if you divide that amount over 20 years, it averages out to around $28,400 per year. The Conners are accustomed to a more significant annual income than that. To make up the difference, they will have to rely on alternative retirement income options. They will basically have to depend on a bigger nest egg to provide them with the income they need.

If they wait until their FRA, they will increase their lifetime benefits to an estimated $609,000. This option allows them to achieve their Primary Insurance Amount, which will provide them a $34,200 annual income.

After learning the Conners' needs and using software to calculate the most optimal time to begin drawing benefits, the Conners' financial professional determined that the best option for them drastically increases their potential lifetime benefits to $649,000!

By using strategies that their financial professional recommended, they increased their potential lifetime benefits by as much as ***$80,000.*** *There's no telling how much you could miss out on from your Social Security if you don't take time to create a strategy that calculates your maximum benefit. For the Conners, the value of maximizing their benefits was the difference between night and day. While this may seem like a special case, it isn't uncommon to find benefit increases of this magnitude. You'll never know unless you take a look at your own options.*

Despite the importance of knowing when and how to take your Social Security benefit, many of today's retirees and pre-retirees may know little about the mechanics of Social Security and how they can maximize their benefit.

So, to whom should you turn for advice when making this complex decision? Before you pick up the phone and call Uncle Sam, you should know that the Social Security Administration (SSA) representatives are actually prohibited from giving you election advice! Plus, SSA representatives in general are trained to focus on monthly benefit amounts, not the lifetime income for a family.

MAXIMIZING YOUR LIFETIME BENEFIT

As discussed in Chapter 2, calculating how to maximize **lifetime benefits** is more important than waiting until age 70 for your maximum **monthly benefit amount**. It's about getting the most income during your lifetime. Professional benefit maximization software can target the year and month that it is most beneficial for you to file based on your life expectancy.

The three most common ages that people associate with retirement benefits are 62 (earliest eligible age), 66 (full retirement age), and 70 (age at which monthly maximum benefit is reached). In almost all circumstances, however, none of those three most common ages will give you the maximum lifetime benefit.

Remember, every month you wait to file, the amount of your benefit check goes up, but you also get one less check. You don't know how exactly how long you're going to live, but you have a better idea of your life expectancy than the actuaries at the Social Security Administration who can only work with averages. They can't make calculations based on your specific situation. A professional can run the numbers for you and get the target date that maximizes your potential lifetime benefits. You can't get this information from the Social Security Administration, but you *can* get it from a financial professional.

Types of Social Security Benefits:
- *Retired Worker Benefit.* This is the benefit with which most people are familiar. The Retired Worker Benefit is what most people are talking about when they refer to Social Security. It is your benefit based on your earnings and the amount that you have paid into the system over the span of your career.
- *Spousal Benefit.* This is available to the spouse of someone who is eligible for Retired Worker Benefits.
- *Survivorship Benefit.* When one spouse passes away, the survivor is able to receive the larger of the two benefit amounts.
- *Restricted Application.* A higher-earning spouse may be able to start collecting a spousal benefit on the lower-earning spouse's benefit while allowing his or her benefit to continue to grow. Due to the Bipartisan Budget Act of 2015, this option is only available to individuals who turned age 62 on or before January 1, 2016.

In November of 2015, the Bipartisan Budget Act of 2015 was passed, which will have a dramatic impact on the way many Americans plan for Social Security. As the largest change to Social Security since 2000, the Bipartisan Budget Act of 2015 eliminated an estimated $9.5 billion* of benefits to retirees and may limit some of the flexibility you previously had to structure your benefits.

In 2000, Congress passed the Senior Citizens Freedom to Work Act. The bill allowed retirees to suspend receiving benefits so they wouldn't be subject to additional taxation if they chose to return to work after they filed for Social Security. However, by

---

* *http://www.nasdaq.com/article/congress-planning-to-close-social-security-loopholes-cm536252*

doing so, the bill also unintentionally created several loopholes in claiming strategies: most notably, the Restricted Application for spousal benefits and "file and suspend" filing strategy. For most Americans, the Bipartisan Budget Act of 2015 closed these loopholes by eliminating "file and suspend" and the Restricted Application.

The new rules mandate that:
- If a primary worker is not currently receiving benefits, then their dependents (child, spouse) can no longer collect benefits based on the primary worker's earning record.
- If you file for benefits, then you are filing for *all* benefits to which you are entitled—not just the benefit type you choose.

It's important to remember that in spite of these immense changes, one thing stayed the same—filing for Social Security is one of the most important financial decisions you will make in your lifetime, and a financial professional can help ensure you make the right one.

THE DIVORCE FACTOR

How does a divorced spouse qualify for benefits? If you have gone through a divorce, it might affect the retirement benefit to which you are entitled.

In general, a person can receive benefits as a divorced spouse on a former spouse's Social Security record so long as the following conditions are met:
- the marriage lasted at least 10 years; and
- the person filing for divorce benefits is at least age 62, unmarried, and not entitled to a higher Social Security benefit on his or her own record.*

---

* http://www.ssa.gov/retire2/yourdivspouse.htm

With all of the different options, strategies and benefits to choose from, you can see why filing for Social Security is more complicated than just mailing in the paperwork. Gathering the data and making yourself aware of all your different options isn't enough to know exactly what to do, however. On the one hand, you can knock yourself out trying to figure out which options are best for you and wondering if you made the best decision. On the other hand, you can work with a financial professional who uses customized software that takes all the variables of your specific situation into account and calculates your best option. You have tens of thousands of different options for filing for your Social Security benefit. If your spouse is a different age than you are, it nearly doubles the amount of options you have. This is far more complicated arithmetic than most people can do on their own. If you want a truly accurate understanding of when and how to file, you need someone who will ask you the right questions about your situation and who has access to specialized software that can crunch the numbers. The reality is that you need to work with a professional that can provide you with the sophisticated analysis of your situation that will help you make a truly informed decision.

Important Questions About Your Social Security Benefit:
- *How can I maximize my lifetime benefit?* By knowing when and how to file for Social Security. This usually means waiting until you have at least reached your Full Retirement Age. A professional has the experience and the tools to help determine when and how you can maximize your lifetime benefits.
- *Who will provide reliable advice for making these decisions?* Only a professional has the tools and experience to provide you reliable advice.

- *Will the Social Security Administration provide me with the advice?* The Social Security Administration cannot provide you with advice or strategies for claiming your benefit. It can give you information about your monthly benefit, but that's it. It also doesn't have the tools to tell you what your specific best option is. It can accurately answer questions about how the system works, but it can't advise you about what decision to make as to how and when to file for benefits.

These specialized software programs are an invaluable resource that can help you understand how and when to file for your Social Security benefit. Not only can they help you better understand all the options available to you—but they can help you understand the financial implications of each choice.

CHAPTER 4 TAKE-AWAY //
- It takes a professional who understands tax law and Social Security strategies, utilizing a customized Maximization Report in order to optimize your Social Security benefit in a way that's specific to your individual situation.

5
FILLING THE INCOME GAP

"A scientist can discover a new star, but he cannot make one. He would have to ask an engineer to do that."
– Gordon L. Glegg, British Engineer, 1969

As a retiree, income is the star of your portfolio. Without income, the future of your retirement is left in the dark, because you can't spend your money with any degree of certainty unless you know your basic expenses are secured and guaranteed for life. Most investors realize that living off the stock market is not an ideal way to fill their income gap, but they aren't aware of what their other options are. If you have a known income gap to fill, then you are probably looking for an investment that can give you the following:

- Guarantees

- Growth
- Lifetime income

There is a way to get all three using a newer kind of annuity referred to in this book as *an income annuity*. This can be a tough decision for some people, however, because the word annuity has gotten a lot of negative attention and marketing. Furthermore, there are some kinds of annuities out there sold to retirees that DONT give you the benefits mentioned above. Variable annuities, for example, are Red Money investments that don't give the same guarantees. This chapter is designed to help you overcome your fear of annuities so can take advantage of the many benefits offered by today's newer fixed indexed annuity options.

TAKING A GUARANTEED APPROACH TO YOUR INCOME NEEDS

You looked at Social Security strategies earlier, discovering you have some control over how and when you file. Those decisions can change the outcome of your benefit in your favor. Once you start drawing that income, it is safer and will provide you with a reliable source of income for the rest of your life. While there are many factors of Social Security that you can control, there are many that you cannot.

For example, you do not have the choice of putting more money into Social Security in order to get more out of it. If you could have the option to contribute more money toward Social Security in order to secure a guaranteed income, it would be a great way to create a Green Money asset that would enhance your retirement. Since that option isn't available, you may seek an investment tool that is similar to Social Security that provides you with a reliable income. It also has the potential to increase the value of your principal investment! This kind of win-win situation exists, and it's called an income annuity.

Today, you probably have savings in a variety of assets that you acquired over the years. But you may not have taken time to examine them and assess how they will support your retirement. It's not about whether the market goes up or down, but when it does. If it goes down at the wrong time for your five or 10 year retirement horizon, you could be in serious danger of losing some of your retirement income.

If you have assets that you would like to structure for retirement income, **an income annuity may be the right choice for you.**

Annuities are popular and reliable investment tools that allow you to secure income during retirement, but they can be used in other ways as well. Income annuities with indexing features such as the type discussed in this chapter can be used in three different ways:
1. To create a guaranteed income.
2. To safely accumulate or grow money not needed for income.
3. To grow money for your spouse or beneficiaries for later use.

In its simplest form, an annuity is a way to invest your money for the long-term, and when purchased with an income rider, you can structure the money so that it delivers a guaranteed stream of income. Annuities come in a variety of modes. Finding the right one for you will take a conversation with your financial professional. Be sure you fully understand the features, benefits and costs of any annuity you are considering before investing money.

HOW AN INCOME ANNUITY CAN FIT INTO AN INCOME PLAN

If you are concerned about the best way to fill your income gap or to safely grow your money for later needs, an income annuity is likely a good option for you. Income annuities have many similar qualities to Social Security that give them the same look and feel as that reliable benefit check you get every month. Most importantly, an income annuity can be an efficient and profitable way to solve your income gap.

Ask yourself the following questions:
- How concerned are you about finding a secure financial vehicle to protect your savings?
- How concerned are you that there may be a better way to structure your savings?
- Would you like to have a Green Money strategy that allows you to capture market gains without being exposed to market loss?

If you are concerned about the best way to fill your income gap, an income annuity with an income rider might be a good option for you. If you want to plan for your spouse, grow your money for ten or more years down the road, or plan for your legacy, then you might use an indexed annuity with a death benefit rider to create guarantees within your portfolio. This is a popular and versatile investment that can give you and your spouse a guaranteed lifetime income while also helping to address future concerns such as inflation and legacy.

Here is how they can work:
When you put your money into an annuity, you are essentially buying an investment product from an insurance company. It is a contract between you and the insurance company that provides the investment tool. Let's say you have saved $100,000 and need it to generate income to meet your needs above and beyond your Social Security and pension checks. You give the $100,000 to an insurance company, who in turn invests it to generate growth.

They usually select investments that have modest returns over long term horizons. In other words, they generally put it somewhere stable and predictable. Most commonly, they will invest it in a combination of bonds and treasuries that are safer and dependable ways to grow money. They use the money from the insurance products they sell to invest, use a portion of the returns to generate profits for themselves, and return a portion to clients in the form of payouts, claims, and structured income options.

One of the most attractive qualities of these types of annuities is something called annual reset. Annual reset is sometimes also referred to as a "ratcheting." Instead of taking on the risk that comes with putting money in a fluctuating market, you can offset that risk onto the insurance company. When you use that $100,000 to buy a contract with an insurance company in the form of an annuity, you are **pegging your money on an index**. It could be the S&P 500, the Dow Jones Industrial Average or any number of indexes. It works like this:

If the market goes down, you don't suffer a loss. Instead, the insurance company absorbs it.

If the market goes up, you share with the insurance company some of the profit made on the gain. The amount of gain you get is called your annuity participation rate. Typically the insurer will cap the amount of gain you can realize at somewhere between 3 and 7 percent. If the market goes up 10 percent, you would realize a portion of that gain (whatever percentage you are capped at). This means **you never lose money on your investment, while always gaining a portion of the upswings**. The measurement period of your annuity can be calculated monthly, weekly and even daily, but most annuities are measured annually. The level of the index when you buy and the index level one year later will determine the amount of loss or gain. You and the insurance company are betting that the market will generally go up over time. The following example shows just how helpful an income annuity option can be for a retiree:

> » Barry and Karen are 62 years old and have decided to run the numbers to see what their retirement is going to look like. They know they currently need $6,000 per month to pay their bills and maintain their current lifestyle. They have also done their Social Security homework and have determined that, between the two of them, they will receive $4,200 per month in benefits. They also receive $350 per month in rent from a tenant who lives in a small carriage house in their backyard. Between their Social Security and the monthly rent income, they will be short $1,450 per month.
>
> They do have an additional asset, however. They have been contributing for years to an IRA that has reached a value of $350,000. They realize that they have to figure out how to turn the $350,000 in their IRA into $1,450 per month for the rest of their life. At first glance, it may seem like they will have plenty of money. With some quick calculations, they find they have 240 months, or nearly 20 years, of monthly income before they exhaust the account. When you consider income tax, the potential for higher taxes in the future, and market fluctuations (because many IRAs are invested in the market), the amount in the IRA seems to have a little less clout. Every dollar Barry and Karen take out of the IRA is subject to income tax, and if they leave the remainder in the IRA, they run the risk of losing money in a volatile market. Once they retire and stop getting a paycheck every two weeks, they also stop contributing to their IRA. And when they aren't supplementing its growth with their own money, they are entirely dependent on market growth. That's a scary prospect. They could also withdraw the money from the IRA and put it in a savings account or CD, but removing all the money

at once will put them in a tax bracket that will claim a huge portion of the value of the IRA. A seemingly straightforward asset has now become a complicated equation. Barry and Karen didn't know what to do, so they met with their financial professional.

Their financial professional suggested that they use the money to purchase an indexed annuity with an income rider. They selected an annuity that was designed for their specific situation. They took the lump sum from their IRA, placed it in an indexed annuity taking advantage of annual reset so they never lost the value of their investment. In return, they were guaranteed the $1,450 of income per month that they needed to meet their retirement goals. The simplicity of the contract allowed them to do an analysis with their professional just once to understand the product. They basically put their money in an investment crockpot where they didn't have to look at it or manage it. They just needed to let it simmer. In fact, their professional was able to find an annuity for them that allowed them their $1,450 monthly payment with a lump sum of $249,455, leaving them more than $100,000 to reinvest somewhere else. Keep in mind that annuities are tax deferred, meaning you will pay tax on the income you receive from an annuity in the year you receive it.

THE INNER WORKINGS OF INCOME RIDERS

When you use that $100,000 to buy a contract with an insurance company in the form of an annuity, you are pegging your money on an index. It could be the S&P 500, the Dow Jones Industrial Average or any number of indexes. To generate income from the annuity, you select something called an income rider. An income rider is a subset of an indexed annuity. Essentially, it is the amount of money from which the insurance company will pay you an income while you have your money in their annuity. Your income rider is a larger number than what your investment is actually worth, and if you select the income rider, it will increase in value over time, providing you with more income. As the insurance company holds your money and invests it, they generate a return on it that they use to pay you a regular monthly income based on a higher number. The insurance company has to outperform the amount that they pay you in order to make a profit.

Remember, insurance companies make long-term investments that provide them with predictable flows of money.

They like to stabilize the amount of money that goes in and out of their doors instead of paying and receiving large unpredictable chunks at once. When you opt for an income rider, an insurance company can reliably predict how much money they will pay out to you over a set period of time. It's predictable, and they like that. They can base their business on those predictable numbers.

In order to encourage investors to leave their money in their annuity contracts, insurance companies create surrender periods that protect their investments. If you remove your money from the annuity contract during the surrender period, you will pay a penalty and will not be able to receive your entire investment amount back. A typical surrender period is 10 years. If after three years you decide that you want your $100,000 back, the insurance company has that money tied up in bonds and other investments with the understanding that they will have it for another seven years. Because they will take a hit on removing the money from their investments prematurely, you will have to pay a surrender charge that makes up for their loss. During the surrender period, an annuity is not a demand deposit account like a savings or checking account. The higher returns that you are guaranteed from an annuity are dependent on the timeframe you selected. The longer an insurance company can hold your money, the easier it is for them to guarantee a predictable return on it.

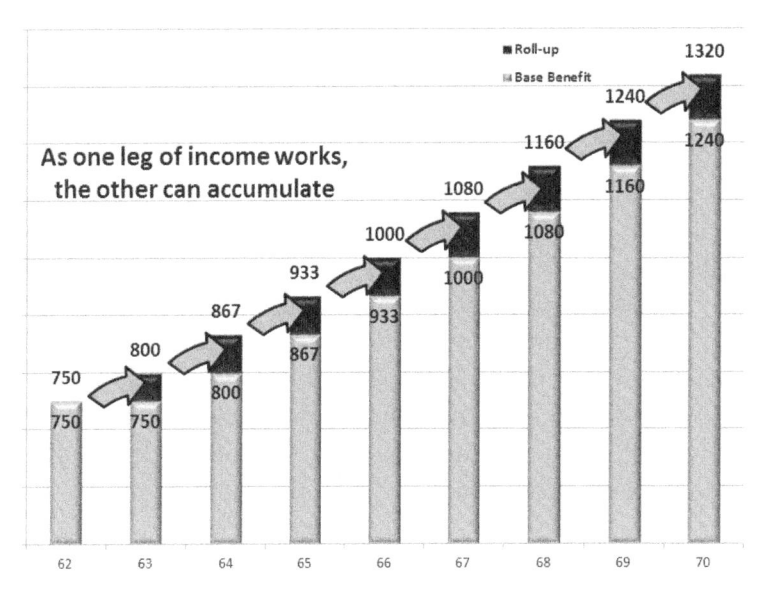

As one leg of income works, the other can accumulate

This is a hypothetical illustration

If you leave your money in the annuity contract, you get a reliable monthly income no matter what happens in the market. Once the surrender period has expired, you can remove your money whenever you want. Your money becomes liquid again because the insurance company has used it in an investment that fit the timeline of your surrender period. For many people, this is an attractive trade off that can provide a creative solution for filling their income gap.

When is an annuity with an income rider right for you? A good financial professional can help you make that determination by taking the time to listen closely to your situation and understanding what your needs are as you enter retirement. Every salesperson has a bag full of brochures and PowerPoint presentations, but they need to know exactly what the financial concerns of their individual clients are in order to help them make the most informed and beneficial decision. Some people need income today, others need it in five or 10 years. Others may have their income needs met but are planning to move closer to their children and will need to buy a house in 10 years. Or, if you want income in 15 years, you might want to choose a different investment product for 10 years, and then switch to an annuity with an income rider during the last five years of your timeline. Everyone's situation is different and everyone's needs are different. People who are interested in annuities, however, usually need to make decisions that affect their income needs, whether it is filling their income gap, or providing for income down the road.

What happens if you place on a shorter timeframe those assets from which you need to draw an income? Something called single premium immediate annuities may be for you:

SINGLE PREMIUM IMMEDIATE ANNUITIES (SPIA)

A single premium immediate annuity is simply a contract between you and an insurance company. SPIAs are structured so that you pay a lump sum of money (a single premium) to an insurance company, and they give you a guaranteed income over an agreed upon time period. That time period could be five years, or it could be for the remainder of your lifetime. Guarantees from insurance companies are based on the claims-paying ability of the issuing insurance company.

SPIAs provide investors with a stream of reliable income when they can't afford to take the risk of losing money in a fluctuating market. While there is general faith that the market always trends up, at least in the long-term, if you are focusing on income over a shorter period of time, you may not be able to take a big hit in the market. Beyond normal market volatility, interest rates also come with an inherent level of uncertainty, making it hard to create a dependable income on your own. SPIAs reduce risk for you by giving you regular monthly, quarterly or yearly payments that can begin the moment you buy the contract. Your financial professional can walk you through a series of different payment options to help you select the one that most closely fits your needs.

Additional Annuity Information:
- Some contracts will allow you to draw income from the high water mark that the market reaches each year. The income rider will then begin calculating its value from the high water mark.
- Variable annuities, however, can lose money with market fluctuations. As their name suggests, they vary with the market. These annuities do not take advantage of annual reset when the market goes down. The income rider will stay the same, but the value of your actual contract may fall. If you surrender the annuity, the insurance company will pay you the market value of the asset, regardless of whether it matches, exceeds or falls short of the value at which you bought the contract. If its value has dropped significantly, you may be better off taking the income rider without surrendering your contract.
- Income annuities are investment tools that look and feel a bit like Social Security. Every year you allow the money to grow with the market, and it will "roll up" by a specific amount, paying out a specific percent to you as income each year.
- Annuities can work very well to create income, and a financial professional can help you find the one that best matches your income need, and can also structure it to work perfectly for you.

Managing Risk Within Your Annuity:
Just like any investment strategy, the amount of risk needs to fit the comfort level of the investor. Annuities are no exception.

Without going into too much detail, here are some additional ways to manage risk with annuity options:
- If you want to structure an annuity investment for growth over a long period of time, you can select a variable annuity. The value of your principal investment follows the market and can lose or gain value with the market. This type of annuity can also have an income rider, but it is really more useful as an accumulation tool that bets on an improving market. A 40-year-old couple, for example, will probably want to structure more for growth and take on more risk than someone in their 70s. The 40-year-old couple may select a variable annuity with an income rider that kicks in when they plan to retire. If it rises with the market or outperforms it, the value of their investment has grown. If the market loses ground over the duration of the contract or their annuity underperforms, they can still rely on the income rider.
- If you are 68 years old and you have more immediate income needs that you need to come up with above and beyond your Social Security, you need a low risk, reliable source of income. If you choose an annuity option, you are looking for something that will pay out an income right away over a relatively short timeframe. You probably want to opt for a SPIA that pays you immediately and spans a five year period, as well as an additional annuity that begins paying you in five years, and another longer term annuity that begins paying you in 10 years. Bear in mind that each annuity contract has its own costs and fees. Review these with your financial professional before you determine the best products and strategies for your situation.

FILLING THE INCOME GAP

The following example shows just how helpful an indexed annuity option with an income rider can be for a retiree who has a known income gap that needs to be filled:

> » *Candy is 60 years old and is wondering how she can use her assets to provide her with a retirement income. She has a $5,000 per month income need. If she starts withdrawing her Social Security benefit in six years at age 66, it will provide her with $2,200 per month. She also has a pension that kicks in at age 70 that will give her another $1,320 per month.*
>
> *That leaves an income gap of $2,800 from ages 66 to 69, and then an income gap of $1,480 at age 70 and beyond. If Candy uses only Green Money to solve her income need, she will need to deposit $918,360 at 2 percent interest to meet her monthly goal for her lifetime. If she opts to use Red Money and withdraws the amount she needs each month from the market, let's say the S & P 500, she will run out of cash in 10 years if she invested between the years of 2000 and 2012. Suffering a market downturn like that during the period for which she is relying on it for retirement income will change her life, and not for the better.*
>
> *Working with a financial professional to find a better way, Candy found that she could take a hybrid approach to fill her income gap. Her professional recommended two different income vehicles: one that allowed her to deposit just $190,161 with a 2 percent return, and one that was a $146,000 income annuity. These tools filled her income gap with $336,161, requiring her to spend $582,000 less money to accomplish her goal! Working with a professional to find the right tools for her retirement needs saved Candy over half a million dollars.*

CREATING AN INCOME PLAN

Creating an income plan before you retire allows you to satisfy your need for lifetime income and ensures that your lifestyle can last as long as you do. You also want to create a plan that operates in the most efficient way possible. Doing so will give more security to your Need Later Money and will potentially allow you to build your legacy down the road.

Here is a basic roadmap of what we have covered so far:
- Review your income needs and look specifically at the shortfall you may have during each year of your retirement based on your Social Security income, and income from any other assets you have.
- Ask yourself where you are in your distribution phase. Is retirement one year away? 10 years away? Last year?
- Determine how much money you need and how you need to structure your existing assets to provide for that need.
- If you have an asset from which you need to generate income, consider options offered by purchasing an income rider on an annuity.

CHAPTER 5 TAKE-AWAY //
- Do you want your base income needs guaranteed, or exposed to risk and dependent on market performance of the stock market? If you want them guaranteed, an insurance company can fill your income gap using fixed, indexed and income annuities so you can know your base needs will be met during retirement.

6

THE HOUSE MADE OF CARDS:
A WRONG WAY TO INVEST DURING RETIREMENT

"When you want to know how things really work, study them when they're coming apart."
– William Gibson, Zero History

You've built a strong foundation for your retirement plan by optimizing your Social Security benefit, filling the income gap and making an effort to truly diversify your portfolio. Once you have worked with a financial professional to structure your income needs, it's time to take a look at the future. With your immediate income needs met, you have the opportunity to take your additional assets and leverage them for profit to supplement your income in the future, to prepare for anticipated health care costs or to contribute to your legacy. Stable income also means that you should have the staying power to stick with your investment portfolio through the ups and downs in the market.

The question is, **what kind of investment structure will you build on top of your strong foundation?** A house of bricks (a strong strategy), a house made of sticks (reasonably strong), or a house made of cards? Obviously, no one would intentionally choose to build themselves a house of cards to live in if they knew that's what they were doing. Most people don't realize that the typical diversification and distribution strategies employed by large brokerage firms are *not engineered* to protect someone in retirement during today's volatile and unpredictable times.

We made the point earlier that the tactics you employed when investing during your working years should likely change once you enter the distribution phase of your life. One of the biggest reasons for this has to do with a mathematical concept known as the Sequence of Returns. This has been the demise of many retirees who worked and saved a lifetime, only to start their retirement during a bad year on Wall Street. Their distribution plans came apart, and the information included in this chapter is here to show you exactly WHY so you can engineer a better plan.

THE SEQUENCE OF RETURNS

Here is a simple fact that the average investor isn't aware of: stock market returns affect your investment differently when you're taking income during your retirement years than they did during your working years. The reason for this has to do with both *the amount of loss* and *when the loss occurs.* **The Sequence of Returns refers to the order that your gains and losses are calculated.** No one knows exactly what the stock market will be doing a year from now, two years from now, or even 10 years from now. It could be up or it could be down. During your working years, how

THE HOUSE MADE OF CARDS: A WRONG WAY TO INVEST DURING RETIREMENT

does the order of the returns affect your portfolio balance? Let's take a look.

SEQUENCE OF RETURNS DURING YOUR WORKING YEARS:

When you are in your accumulation years, working and earning a paycheck from your job, you are able to leave your investment accounts (for the most part) alone. You don't need to use the money in your accumulation accounts for income because you already have an income, and so you can let these accounts recover when a loss occurs.

Notice in the chart below how we have two investors saving diligently for retirement, both with the exact same portfolio balance of $100,000. The investors are averaging 6 percent returns during a 10 year period. Now take a look at what happens:

Investor A receives a nice big fat 14 percent return his first year investing. Woo-hoo! Investor A is feeling pretty good and he stays in the market. Year two, he is rewarded with a 35 percent return. What a great year! His account is now up to $153,900 and he is definitely staying in the market. Year three isn't as great, but he earns a solid 11 percent. He thinks the market is a great place to be and so he stays in for a total of 10 years.

Investor B, on the other hand, does poorly his first year out of the gate. He earns nothing, his account dropping by a depressing -8 percent, but he's not worried. His broker reminds him they are in this for the long haul, and so Investor B stays in the market. Year two, he does even worse, losing 20 percent. His $100,000 is now down to a meager $73,600. Investor B is starting to get discouraged, but then in year three, he finally earns a positive 2 percent return. He stays in the market for a total of 10 years, and finally, in year nine, he is rewarded with a nice juicy 35 percent return.

Notice how Investor A received nice gains at the beginning of his 10 year period, whereas Investor B received nothing but losses in the beginning. **Their actual returns are exactly the same, the only difference was the order in which they were calculated.** Who do you think has the bigger portfolio at the end of the 10 year period? Does Investor A have the bigger portfolio? Or Investor B?

The answer: They both have exactly same: a portfolio balance of $160,000.

Investor A:

Year	% Return	$100,000
1	-8%	$92,000
2	-20%	$73,600
3	2%	$75,072
4	-5%	$71,318
5	8%	$77,024
6	28%	$98,591
7	-5%	$93,661
8	11%	$103,964
9	35%	$140,351
10	14%	$160,000
Average	6%	$160,000

Investor B:

Year	% Return	$100,000
1	14%	$114,000
2	35%	$153,900
3	11%	$170,829
4	-5%	$162,288
5	28%	$207,728
6	8%	$224,346
7	-5%	$213,129
8	2%	$217,392
9	-20%	$173,913
10	-8%	$160,000
Average	6%	$160,000

Surprised? The lesson we learn here is that during your accumulation years, the order or sequence of your returns doesn't matter.

Now let's compare this to what happens during your distribution years.

WHEN THINGS FALL APART

Once again we have two investors who are starting out with the exact same account balance earning the exact same rate of return. The only difference is that these two investors are retired, and just like in real life, each of these investors chose to retire at a different point in time. Because this story uses the average annual return rates from the S&P 500, we're going to name our investors Larry and Sam. Let's take a look at what happens:

Both Larry and Sam have saved diligently and enter into retirement with a portfolio balance of $300,000. Both Larry and Sam are working with a broker who has them withdrawing 4 percent annually to receive their income of $12,000. This example also covers a 10-year time span in the life of our intrepid investors, and the returns are calculated based on the annual returns of the S&P 500 index from 1997 to 2007.* Let's take a look at how they fair:

Lucky Larry: In 1997, Larry withdraws his $12,000 and receives a 31.01 percent return. Good for Larry! His ending account balance is $381,030, which is just what he hopes to see. In 1998, things are still looking good. He takes out his $12,000 and earns another 26.67 percent; his account balance is a healthy $470,291. In 1999 he sees another gain of 19.53 percent; in the year 2000, things start to go south. As we all experienced, the year 2001 was terrible, and things don't look up again until 2003.

Sorry Sam: Now let's take a moment to check-in with Sam. He is a few years younger than Larry, and so he retires in the year 2000 instead of the year 1997. Sam retires with the $300,000 he worked all his life to save. Following the 4 percent distribution plan designed by his broker, Sam starts taking his $12,000 withdrawals, and then—cue the music of doom—disaster strikes. He loses 10.14 percent in 2000, another 13.04 percent in 2001, and a devastating loss of 23.37 percent in 2002. Sam is feeling

---

* *Finance.yahoo.com*

pretty sorry. He is looking around, wondering, *what the heck just happened?*

Now, continuing this trend, who do you think has a bigger portfolio balance at the end of ten years?

If you guessed that they are again both the same, then you guessed wrong. The Sequence of Returns can make or break a perfectly good retirement. **When you look at the math, it will show you that it's NOT the average rate of return or even the size of your portfolio that matters during your distribution years, it's WHEN you retire that dictates how well your portfolio will perform.** Larry is lucky. He retired, and then had three years of gains. His portfolio balance is $406,906. He also went through the three bad years of 2000, 2001 and 2002, but things worked out for Larry, which is why we call him lucky.

Did he save more than Sam? Nope.

Invest differently? Nope.

Take out less money? Use a special strategy? Hire a Life Coach? Nope. Lucky Larry didn't do anything special. He just retired in the right year.

Sequence of Returns - Distribution

Investment Amount: $300,000   Withdraw Rate: 4%

"LUCKY LARRY"				"SORRY SAM"			
Balance	Annual Return*	Annual Withdrawal	End Balance	Balance	Annual Return*	Annual Withdrawal	End Balance
1997 300,000	31.01%	12,000	381,030	2000 300,000	-10.14%	12,000	257,580
1998 381,030	26.67%	12,360	470,291	2001 257,580	-13.04%	12,360	211,632
1999 470,291	19.53%	12,731	549,408	2002 211,632	-23.37%	12,731	149,442
2000 549,408	-10.14%	13,113	480,585	2003 149,442	26.38%	13,113	175,753
2001 480,585	-13.04%	13,506	404,411	2004 175,753	8.99%	13,506	178,047
2002 404,411	-23.37%	13,911	295,989	2005 178,047	3.00%	13,911	169,477
2003 295,989	26.38%	14,329	359,742	2006 169,477	13.62%	14,329	178,231
2004 359,742	8.99%	14,758	377,324	2007 178,231	3.52%	14,758	169,746
2005 377,324	3.00%	15,201	373,443	2008 169,746	-38.47%	15,201	89,244
2006 373,443	13.62%	15,657	408,648	2009 89,244	23.48%	15,657	94,541
2007 408,648	3.52%	16,127	406,906	2010 94,541	12.55%	16,127	90,279

$406,906   **$90,279**

*Annual returns of S&P 500 index. Source: finance.yahoo.com

Leaving your retirement in the hands of the stock market is not necessarily in your best interest. You obviously can't control what the market will do, and you also might not have a lot of choice when it comes to the year in which you retire. **The only thing you can control is how well you will plan.**

Relying on outdated strategies such as the 4 percent rule as the foundation for your distribution plan is like building a house made of cards and then moving in, expecting to enjoy a nice long retirement.

There's no way your house of cards can withstand the huff and puff of a big-bad downturn, unless, of course, you happen to be like Lucky Larry.

You don't have to leave it up to luck, chance or the big-bad wolf. You can chose instead to secure your income needs first, build yourself a house of bricks, and then kick back and let the winds howl.

HOW TO BUILD A HOUSE OF CARDS

It can be challenging to watch the stock market's erratic changes every month, week or even every day. When you have your money riding on it, the ride can feel pretty bumpy. When you are managing your money by yourself, emotions inevitably enter into the mix. The Dow Jones Industrial Average and the S&P 500 represent more to you than market fluctuations. They represent a portion of your retirement. It's hard not to be emotional about it.

Everyone knows you should buy low and sell high. But this is what is more likely to happen:

The market takes a downturn, similar to the 2008 crash, and investors see as much as a 30 percent loss in their stock holdings. It's hard to watch, and it's harder to bear the pain of losing that much money. The math of rebounds means that they will need to rely on even larger gains just to get back to where things were before the downturn. They sell. But eventually, and inevitably, the market begins to rise again. Maybe slowly, maybe with some moderate growth, but by the time the average investor notices an upward trend and wants to buy in again, they have already missed a great deal of the gains. Gloria's situation illustrates how market volatility can have major repercussions for an individual investor who retires without an income strategy in place:

> » *Gloria works for Acme Paper Company for 34 years. During her time there, she acquires bonuses and pay raises that often include shares of stock in the company. She also dedicates part of her paycheck every month to a 401(k) that bought Acme stock. By the time she retires, Gloria has $250,000 worth of Acme stock.*
>
> *Although she had contributes to her 401(k) account every month, Gloria doesn't cultivate any other assets that could generate income for her during retirement. Gloria also retires early at age 62 because of her failing health. The commute to work every day was becoming difficult in her weakened condition and she wanted to enjoy the rest of her life in retirement instead of working at Acme.*
>
> *Because she retires early, Gloria fails to maximize her Social Security benefit. While she lives a modest lifestyle, her income needs will still be $3,500 per month. Gloria's monthly Social Security check will only cover $1,900, leaving her with a $1,600 income gap. To supplement her Social Security check, Gloria sells $1,600 of her Acme stock each month to meet her income needs. A $250,000 401(k) is nothing to sneeze at, but reducing its value by $1,600 every month will barely last Gloria 10 years. And that's if the market stays neutral or grows modestly. If the market takes a downturn, the money that Gloria relied on to fill her income gap will rapidly diminish. Even if the market starts going up in a couple of years, it will take much larger gains for her to recover the value that she lost.*

Unhappily for Gloria, she retired in 2007, just before the major market downturn that lasted for several years. She lost more than 20 percent of the value of her stock. Because Gloria needed to sell her stock to meet her basic income needs, the market price of the stock was secondary to her need for the money. When she needed money, she was forced to sell however many shares she needed to fill her income gap that month. And if she has a financial crisis, involving her need for medical care, for example, she will be forced to sell stock even if the market is low and her shares are nearly worthless.

Gloria realizes that she could have relied on an investment structured to deliver her a regular income while protecting the value of her investment. She could have kept her $250,000 from diminishing while enjoying her lifestyle into retirement regardless of the volatility of the market. Ideally, Gloria would have restructured her 401(k) to reflect the level of risk that she was able to take. In her case, she would have had most of her money in Green Money assets, allowing her to rely on the value of her assets when she needed them.

HOW REAL PEOPLE MAKE INVESTMENT DECISIONS

It can be challenging to watch the stock market's erratic changes every month, week or even every day. When you have your money riding on it, the ride can feel pretty bumpy. When you are managing your money by yourself, emotions inevitably enter into the mix. The Dow Jones Industrial Average and the S&P 500 represent more to you than market fluctuations. They represent a portion of your retirement. It's hard not to be emotional about it.

Everyone knows you should buy low and sell high. But this is what is more likely to happen:

The market takes a downturn, similar to the 2008 crash, and investors see as much as a 30 percent loss in their stock holdings. It's hard to watch, and it's harder to bear the pain of losing that much money. The math of rebounds means that they will need to rely on even larger gains just to get back to where things were before the downturn. They sell. But eventually, and inevitably, the market begins to rise again. Maybe slowly, maybe with some moderate growth, but by the time the average investor notices an upward trend and wants to buy in again, they have already missed a great deal of the gains.

In 2017, DALBAR, the well-respected financial services market research firm, released their annual "Quantitative Analysis of Investment Behavior" report (QAIB). The report studied the impact of market volatility on individual investors: people like Lisa, or anyone who was managing (or mismanaging) their own investments in the stock market.

According to the study, volatility not only caused investors to make decisions based on their emotions, those decisions also harmed their investments and prevented them from realizing potential gains. So why do people meddle so much with their investments when the market is fluctuating? Part of the reason is that many people have financial obligations that they don't have control over. Significant expenses like house payments, the unexpected cost of replacing a broken-down car, and medical bills can put people in a position where they need money. If they need to sell investments to come up with that money, they don't have the luxury of selling when they *want* to. They must sell when they *need* to.

DALBAR's "Quantitative Analysis of Investor Behavior" has been used to measure the effects of investors' buying, selling and mutual fund switching decisions since 1994. The QAIB shows time and time again over nearly a 20-year period that the average investor earns less, and in many cases, significantly less than the performance of mutual funds suggests. QAIB's goal is to improve independent investor performance and to help financial professionals provide helpful advice and investment strategies that address the concerns and behaviors of the average investor.

An excerpt from the report claims that:

"QAIB offers guidance on how and where investor behaviors can be improved. No matter what the state of the mutual fund industry, boom or bust: Investment results are more dependent on investor behavior than on fund performance. Mutual fund investors who hold on to their investments are more successful than those who time the market.

QAIB uses data from the Investment Company Institute (ICI), Standard & Poor's and Barclays Capital Index Products to compare mutual fund investor returns to an appropriate set of benchmarks.

There are actually three primary causes for the chronic shortfall for both equity and fixed income investors:
1. *Capital not available to invest. This accounts for 25 percent to 35 percent of the shortfall.*
2. *Capital needed for other purposes. This accounts for 35 percent to 45 percent of the shortfall.*
3. *Psychological factors. These account for 45 percent to 55 percent of the shortfall."*

Psychological factors account for a significant portion of the chronic investment return shortfall for both equity and fixed income investors. All too often, investors may make impulsive investment decisions based on irrational emotions, which can lead to buying and selling at the wrong time.

Asset allocation is designed to handle the investment decision-making for the investor, which can materially reduce the shortfall due to psychological factors. Successful asset allocation investing requires investors to act on two critical imperatives:
1. Balance capital preservation and appreciation so that they are aligned with the investor's objective.

2. Select a qualified allocator.

The best way for an investor to determine their risk tolerance is to utilize a risk tolerance assessment. However, these assessments must be accessible and usable. Evaluating allocator quality requires analysis of the allocator's underlying investments, decision making process and whether or not past efforts have produced successful outcomes.

Choosing a top allocator makes a significant difference in the investment results one will achieve. Mutual fund retention rates suggest that the average investor has not remained invested for long enough periods to derive the potential benefits of the investment markets.

The key findings of DALBAR's QAIB report provide compelling statistics about how individual investment strategies produced negative outcomes for the majority of investors:
- In five out of 12 months, investors guessed right about the market direction the following month. While "guessing right" 42 percent of the time in 2016, the average mutual fund investor was not able to keep pace with the market, based on the actual volume and timing of fund flows
- When looking at the long-term annualized returns of the average equity mutual fund investor compared to the S&P 500 we see that the average investor has always lagged the overall market. While the gap between the average equity mutual fund investor and the S&P 500 has narrowed considerably in the past 15 years, the average investor has earned almost half of what they would have earned by buying and holding an S&P index fund (4.67 percent vs. 8.19 percent).
- No evidence has been found to link predictably poor investment recommendations to average investor underperformance. Analysis of the underperformance shows

that investor behavior is the number one cause, with fees being the second leading cause.
- In 2016, the average equity mutual fund investor underperformed the S&P 500 by a margin of 4.70 percent.*

It doesn't take a financial services market research report to tell you that market volatility is out of your control. The report does prove, however, that before you experience market volatility, you should have an investment plan, and when the market is fluctuating, you should stand by your investment plan. You should also review and discuss your investment plan with your financial professional on a regular basis, ensuring he/she is aware of any changes in your goals, financial circumstances, your health or your risk tolerance. When the economy is under stress and the markets are volatile, investors can feel vulnerable. That vulnerability causes people to tinker with their portfolios in an attempt to outsmart the market. Financial professionals, however, don't try to time the market for their clients. They try to tap into the gains that can be realized by committing to long-term investment strategies.

CHAPTER 6 TAKE-AWAY //
- The Sequence of Returns tells us that all things equal, the order of your returns **does not** matter during your working "accumulation" years, however, **it DOES matter** during your retirement "distribution" years.

2017 QAIB, Dalbar, March 2017

7

THE HOUSE MADE OF BRICKS:
TACTICAL MONEY MANAGEMENT

"One man's "magic" is another man's engineering."
– Robert A. Heinlein

Now that you've calculated the Rule of 100, determined how much risk you have and how much you want, and you've determined how much Green Money you need to meet your short-term and mid-term income needs, it's time to look at what you have left. The money you have left after you've calculated your Green Money needs has the potential of becoming Red Money: your stocks, mutual funds and other investment products that you want to continue accumulating value with the market. You now have the luxury of taking a closer second look at your Red Money to determine how you would like to manage it. As you read earlier in the key findings of the DALBAR report, the deck is stacked against the individual investor. Remember that the average investor failed to keep pace with the market, meaning the inherent risk in managing your Red Money is very real and could have a lasting impact on your assets. So, how much of your Red Money do you invest, and in what kinds of markets, investment products and stocks do you invest? There are a lot of different directions in which you can take your Red Money. One thing is for sure: significant accumulation depends on investing in the market. How you go about doing it is different for everyone. Gathering stocks, bonds and investment funds together in a portfolio without a cohesive strategy behind them could cause you to miss out on the benefits of a more thoughtful and planful approach. The end result is that you may never really understand what your money is doing, where and how it is really invested, and which investment principles are behind the investment products you hold. While you may have goals for each individual piece of your portfolio, it is likely that you don't have a comprehensive plan for your Red Money, which may mean that *you are taking on more risk than you would like, and are getting less return for it than is possible.*

Enter **Yellow Money.** Yellow Money is money that is managed by a professional *with a purpose*. After your income needs are met and you have assets that you would like to dedicate to accumulation, there are decisions you need to make about how to invest those assets. You can buy stocks, index funds, mutual funds, bonds—you name it—you can invest in it. However, the difference between Red Money and Yellow Money is that Yellow Money has a cohesive strategy behind it that is *implemented by a professional*. When you manage your Red Money with an investment plan, it becomes Yellow Money: *money that is being managed* *with a specific purpose, a specific set of focused goals and a specific strategy in mind.* Yellow Money is still a type of Red Money. It comes with different levels of risk. But Yellow Money is under the watchful eye of professionals who have a stake in the success of your money in the market and who can recommend a range of strategies from those designed for preservation to those targeting rapid growth. You don't want to miss out on achieving the right level of risk, and more importantly, composing a careful plan for the return of your assets.

It can be helpful to think of Red Money and Yellow Money with this analogy:

If you needed to travel through an unfamiliar city in a foreign country, you could rent a car or perhaps hire a driver. Were you to drive yourself, you would try to gain guidance from perplexing road signs and need to adhere to traffic rules—with no experience or assistance to lean on. It would take longer to get to where you want to go, and the chance of a traffic accident would be higher. If you hired a driver, they would manage your journey. A driver would know the route, how to avoid traffic, and follow the rules of the road.

Red Money is like driving yourself. With Yellow Money, you are still traveling by car, but now you have a professional working on your behalf.

TAKING A CLOSER LOOK AT YOUR PORTFOLIO

Think about your investment portfolio. Think specifically of what you would consider your Red Money. Do you know what is there? You may have several different investment products like individual mutual funds, bond accounts, stocks, etc. You may have inherited a stock portfolio from a relative, or you might be invested in a bond account offered by the company for which you worked due to your familiarity with them. While you may or may not be managing your investments individually, the reality is that you probably don't have an overall management strategy for all of your investments. Investments that aren't managed are simply Red Money, or money that is at risk in the market. Harnessing the earning potential of your Red Money relies on more than a collection of stocks and bonds, however. It needs guided management. A good Yellow Money manager uses the knowledge they have about the level of risk with which you are comfortable, what you need or want to use your money for, when you want or need it and how you want to use it. The Yellow Money objects that they choose for you will still have a certain level of risk, but under the right management, control and process, you have a far better chance of a successful outcome that meets your specific needs.

When you sit down with an investment professional, you can look at all of your assets together. Chances are that you have accumulated a number of different assets over the last 20, 30 or 50 years. You may have a 401(k), an IRA, a Roth IRA, an account of self-directed stocks, a brokerage account, etc. Wherever you put your money, a financial professional will go through your assets and help you determine the level of risk to which you are exposed now and should be exposed in the future.

Here is a typical example of how an investment professional can be helpful to a future retiree with Yellow Money needs:

> » *Julia is 65 years old and wants to retire in two years. She has a 401(k) from her job to which she has contributed for 26 years. She also has some stocks that her late husband managed. Julia also has $55,000 in a mutual fund that her sister recommended to her five years ago and $30,000 in another mutual fund that she heard about at work. She takes a look at her assets one day and decides that she doesn't understand what they add up to or what kind of retirement they will*

provide. She decides to meet with an investment professional. Julia's professional immediately asks her:

1. Does she know exactly where all of her money is? *Julia doesn't know much about all her husband's stocks, which have now become hers. Their value is at $100,000 invested in three large cap companies. Julia is unsure of the companies and whether she should hold or sell them.*

2. Does she know what types of assets she owns? *Yes and no. She knows she had a 401(k) and IRAs, but she is unfamiliar with her husband's self-directed stock portfolio or the type of mutual funds she owns. Furthermore she is unclear as to how to manage the holdings as she nears retirement.*

3. Does she know the strategies behind each one of the investment products she owns? *While Julia knows she had a 401(k), an IRA and mutual fund holdings, she doesn't know how her 401(k) is organized or how to make it more conservative as she nears retirement. She is unsure whether her IRA is a Roth or traditional variety and how to draw income from them? She really does not have specific investment principles guiding her investment decisions, and she doesn't know anything about her husband's individual stocks. One major concern for Julia is whether her family would be okay if she were not around?*

After determining Julia's assets, her financial professional prepares a consolidated report that lays out all of her assets for her to review. Her professional explains each one of them to her. Julia discovers that although she is two years away from retiring, her 401(k) is organized with an amount of risk with which she is not comfortable. Sixty percent of her 401(k) is at risk, far off the mark if we abide by the Rule of 100. Julia opts to be more conservative than the Rule of 100 suggests, as she will rely on her 401(k) for most of her immediate income needs after retirement. Julia's professional also points out several instances of overlap between her mutual funds. Julia learns that while she is comfortable with one of her mutual funds, she does not agree with the management principles of the other. In the end, Julia's professional helps her re-organize her 401(k) to secure her more Green Money for retirement income. Her professional also uses her mutual fund and her husband's stock assets to create a growth oriented investment plan that Julia will rely on for Need Later Money in 15 years when she plans on relocating closer to her children and grandchildren. By creating an overall investment strategy, Julia is able to meet her targeted goals in retirement. Julia's financial professional worked closely with her and her tax professional to minimize the tax impact of any asset sales on Julia's situation.

Like Julia, you may have several savings vehicles: a 401(k), an IRA to which you regularly contribute, some mutual funds to which you make monthly contributions, etc. But what is your *overall investment strategy?* Do you have one in place? Do you want one that will help you meet your retirement goals? Yellow Money looks at *ALL* your accounts and all their different strategies to create a plan that helps them all work together. Your current investment situation may not reflect your wishes. As a matter of fact, it likely doesn't.

You may have a better understanding of your assets than Julia did, but even someone with an investment strategy can benefit from having a financial professional review their portfolio:

» *Chuck is 69 years old. He retired four years ago. He relied on income from an IRA for three years in order to increase his Social Security benefit. He also made significant investments in 36 different mutual funds. He chose to diversify among the funds by selecting a portion for growth, another for good* dividends, another that focused on promising small cap companies and a final portion that work like index funds. All the money that Chuck had in mutual funds he considered Need Later Money that he wanted to rely on in his 80s. After the stock market took a hit in 2008, Chuck lost some confidence in his investments and decided to sit down with a financial professional to see if his portfolio was able to recover.

The professional Chuck met with was able to determine what goals he had in mind. Specifically, the financial professional determined what Chuck actually wanted and needed the money for, and when he needed it. His professional also looked inside each of the mutual funds and discovered several instances of overlap. While Chuck had created diversity in his portfolio by selecting funds focused on different goals, he didn't account for overlap in the companies in which the funds were invested. Out of the 36 funds, his professional found that 20 owned nearly identical stock. While most of the companies were good investments, the high instance of overlap did not contribute to the healthy investment diversity that Chuck wanted. Chuck's financial professional also provided him with a report that explained the concentration ratio of his holdings (noting how much of his portfolio was contained within the top 25 stock holdings), the percentage of his portfolio that each company in which he invested in represented (showing the percentage of net assets that each company made up as an overall position in his portfolio) and the portfolio date of his account (showing when the funds in his portfolio were last updated: as funds are required to report updates only twice per year, it was possible that some of his fund reports could be six months old).

Chuck's professional consolidated his assets into one investment management strategy. This allowed Chuck's investments to be managed by someone he trusted who knew his specific *investment goals and needs. Eliminating redundancy and overlap in his portfolio was easy to do but difficult to detect since Chuck had multiple funds with multiple brokerage firms. Chuck sat down with a professional to see if his mutual funds could perform well, and he left with a consolidated management plan and a money manager that understood him personally. That's Yellow Money at its best.*

AVOIDING EMOTIONAL INVESTING

There's no way around it; people get emotional about their money. And for good reason. You've spent your life working for it, exchanging your time and talent for it, and making decisions about how to invest it, save it and make it grow. The maintenance of your lifestyle and your plans for retirement all depend on it. The best investment strategies, however, don't rely on emotions. One of Yellow Money's greatest strengths lies in the fact that it is managed by someone who understands your needs and desires, but doesn't make decisions about your money under the influence of emotion.

A well-managed investment account meets your goals as a whole, not in individualized and piecemeal ways. Professional money managers do this by creating requirements for each type of investment in which they put your money. We'll call them "screens." Your money manager will run your holdings through the screens they have created to evaluate different types of investment strategies. A professionally managed account will only have holdings that meet the requirements laid out in the overall management plan that was designed to meet your investment goals. The holdings that don't make it through the screens, the ones that don't contribute to your investment goals, are sold and redistributed to investments that your financial professional has determined to be appropriate.

Different screens apply to different Yellow Money strategies. For example, if one of your goals is significant growth, which would require taking on more risk alongside the potential for more return, an investment professional would screen for companies that have high rates of revenue and sales growth, high earnings growth, rising profit margins, and innovative products. On the other hand, if you want your portfolio to be used for income, which would call for lower risk and less return, your professional would screen for dividend yield and sector diversification. *Every investor has a different goal, and every goal requires a customized strategy that uses quantitative screens.* A professional will create a portfolio that reflects your investment desires. If some of the current assets you own complement the strategies that your professional recommends, those will likely stay in your portfolio.

Screening your assets removes emotions from the equation. It removes attachment to underperforming or overly risky investments. Financial professionals aren't married to particular stocks or mutual funds for any reason. They go by the numbers and see your portfolio through a lens shaped by your retirement goals. Your professional understands your wants and needs, and creates an investment strategy that takes your life events and future plans into account. It's a planful approach, and it allows you to tap into the tools and resources of a professional who has built a career around successful investing. Managing money is a full-time job and is best left to a professional money manager.

Removing emotions from investing also allows you to be unaffected by the day-to-day volatility of the market. Your financial professional doesn't ask where the market is going to be in a year, three years or a month from now. If you look at the value of the stock market from the beginning of the twentieth century to today, it's going up. Despite the Great Depression, despite the 1987 crash, despite the 2008 market downturn, the market, as a whole, trends up. Remember the major market downturn in 2008 when the market lost 30 percent of its value? Not only did it completely recover, it has far exceeded its 2008 value. Emotional investing led countless people to sell low as the market went down, and buy the same shares back when the market started to recover. That's an expensive way to do business. While you can't afford to lose money that you need in two, three or five years, your Need Later Money has time to grow. The best way to do so is to make it Yellow.

CREATING AN INVESTMENT STRATEGY

Just like Julia and Chuck, chances are that you can benefit from taking a more managed investment approach tailored to your goals. Yellow Money is generally Need Later Money that you want to grow for needs you'll have in at least 10 years. You can work with your financial planner to create investments that meet your needs within different timeframes. You may need to rely on some of your Yellow Money in 10, 15 or 20 years, whether for additional income, a large purchase you plan on making or a vacation. Whatever you want it for, you will need it down the road. A financial professional can help you rescale the risk of your assets as they grow, helping you lock in your profits and secure a source of income you can depend on later.

So what does a Yellow Money account look like? Here's what it *doesn't* look like: a portfolio with 49 small cap mutual funds, a dozen individual stocks and an assortment of bond accounts. A brokerage account with a hodgepodge of investments, even if goal-oriented, is not a professionally managed account. It's still Red Money. Remember, Yellow Money is a managed account that has an overarching investment philosophy. When you look at making investments that will perform to meet your future income needs, the burning question becomes: How much should you have in the market and how should it be invested? Working with a professional will help you determine how much risk you should take, how to balance your assets so they will meet your goals and how to plan for the big ticket items, like health care expenses, that may be in your future. Yes, Yellow Money is exposed to risk, but by working with a professional, you can manage that risk in a productive way.

WHY YELLOW MONEY?

If you have met your immediate income needs for retirement, why bother with professionally managing your other assets? The money you have accumulated above and beyond your income needs probably has a greater purpose. It may be for your children or grandchildren. You may want to give money to a charity or organization that you admire. In short, you may want to craft your legacy. It would be advantageous to grow your assets in the best manner possible. A financial professional has built a career around managing money in profitable ways. They are experts under the supervision of the organization that they represent.

Turning to Yellow Money also means that you don't have to burden yourself with the time commitment, the stress, and the cost of determining how to manage your money. Yellow Money can help you better enjoy your retirement. Do you want to sit down in your home office every day and determine how to best allocate your assets, or do you want to be living your life while someone else manages your money for you? When the majority of your Red Money is managed with a specific purpose by a financial professional, you don't have to be worrying about which stocks to buy and sell today or tomorrow.

SEEKING FINANCIAL ADVICE: STOCK BROKERS VS. INVESTMENT ADVISOR REPRESENTATIVES

Investors basically have access to two types of advice in today's financial world: advice from stock brokers and advice given by investment advisors. Most investors, however, don't know the difference between types of advice and the people from whom they receive advice. Today, there are two primary types of advice offered to investors: advice given by a commission-based registered representative (brokers) and advice given by fee-based Investment Advisor Representatives. Unfortunately, many investors are not aware that a difference exists; nor have they been explained the distinction between the two types of advice. In a survey taken by TD Ameritrade, the top reasons investors choose to work with an independent registered investment advisor are:*

- Registered Investment Advisors are required, as fiduciaries, to offer advice that is in the best interest of clients
- More personalized service and competitive fee structure offered at a Registered Investment Advisor firm
- Dissatisfaction with full commission brokers

The truth is that there is a great deal of difference between stock brokers and investment advisor representatives. For starters, investment advisor representatives are obligated to act in an investor's best interests in every and all aspect of a financial relationship. Confusion continues to exist among investors struggling to find the best financial advice out there and the most credible sources of advice.

Here is some information to help clear up the confusion so you can find good advice from a professional you can trust:

- Investment advisor representatives have the fiduciary duty to act in a client's best interest at all times with every investment decision they make. Stock brokers and brokerage firms usually do not act as fiduciaries to their investors and are not obligated to make decisions that are entirely in the best interest of their customers. For example, if you

---

*2011 Advisor Sentiment Study, commissioned by TD AMERITRADE. TD Ameritrade, Inc.

decide you want to invest in precious metals, a stock broker would offer you a precious metals account from their firm. An Investment Advisor would find you a precious metals account that is the best fit for you based on the investment strategy of your portfolio.

- Investment advisors give their clients a Form ADV describing the methods that the professional uses to do business. An Investment Advisor also obtains client consent regarding any conflicts of interest that could exist with the business of the professional.
- Stock brokers and brokerage firms are not obligated to provide comparable types of disclosure to their customers.
- Whereas stock brokers and firms routinely earn large profits by trading as principal with customers, Investment Advisors cannot trade with clients as principal (except in very limited and specific circumstances).
- Investment Advisors charge a pre-negotiated fee with their clients in advance of any transactions. They cannot earn additional profits or commissions from their customers' investments without prior consent. Registered Investment Advisors are commonly paid an asset-based fee that aligns their interests with those of their clients. Brokerage firms and stock brokers, on the other hand, have much different payment agreements. Their revenues may increase regardless of the performance of their customers' assets.
- Unlike brokerage firms, where investment banking and underwriting are commonplace, Registered Investment Advisors must manage money in the best interests of their customers. Because Registered Investment Advisors charge set fees for their services, their focus is on their client. Brokerage firms may focus on other aspects of the firm that do not contribute to the improvement of their clients' assets.

- Unlike brokers, Registered Investment Advisors do not get commissions from fund or insurance companies for selling their investment products.

Just to drive home the point, here is what a fiduciary duty to a client means for a Registered Investment Advisor. Registered Investment Advisors must:*
- Always act in the best interest of their client and make investment decisions that reflect their goals.
- Identify and monitor securities that are illiquid.
- When appropriate, employ fair market valuation procedures.
- Observe procedures regarding the allocation of investment opportunities, including new issues and the aggregation of orders.
- Have policies regarding affiliated broker-dealers and maintenance of brokerage accounts.
- Disclose all conflicts of interest.
- Have policies on use of brokerage commissions for research.
- Have policies regarding directed brokerage, including step-out trades and payment for order flow.
- Abide by a code of ethics.

CHAPTER 7 TAKE-AWAY //
- Tactical investing strategies used by money managers rely on proven methods and computer algorithms rather than emotions; this can make Red Money less dangerous for someone who is planning to enter or already enjoying their distribution years.

---

* *2011 Advisor Sentiment Study, commissioned by TD AMERITRADE. TD Ameritrade, Inc.*

8

THE THREE PILLARS OF INVESTING:
LIQUIDITY, SAFETY AND RETURN

"To the optimist, the glass is half full. To the pessimist, the glass is half empty. To the engineer, the glass is twice as big as it needs to be."
– Unknown

Earlier, we discussed how today's investment options require advice that is relevant to today. Traditional, outdated investment strategies are not only ineffective, they can be harmful to the average investor. One of the most traditional ways of thinking about investing is the risk versus reward trade-off. It goes something like this:

- Investment options that are considered safer carry less risk, but also offer the potential for less return.

- Riskier investment options carry the burden of volatility and a greater potential for loss, but they also offer a greater potential for large rewards.

Most professionals move their clients back and forth along this range, shifting between investments that are safer and investments that are structured for growth. Essentially, the old rules of investing dictate that you can either choose relative safety *or* return, but you can't have both.

Updated investment strategies work with the flexibility of liquidity to remake the rules. Liquidity refers to your ability to easily access your money. You might think of liquidity as the water in the glass. Do you have too much, too little, or wasted space in your accounts? When you engineer a plan, you can use the three pillars of liquidity, safety and return to get more efficient returns out of your safe investments. Here is how:

There are three dimensions that are inherent in any investment: *Liquidity, Safety,* and *Return*. You can maximize any two of these dimensions at the expense of the third. If you choose Safety and Liquidity, this is like keeping your assets in a checking account or savings account. This option delivers a lot of Safety and Liquidity, but at the expense of any Return. On the other hand, if you choose Liquidity and Return, meaning you have the potential for great return and can still reclaim your money whenever you choose, you will likely be exposed to a very high level of risk.

Understanding Liquidity can help you break the old Risk versus Safety trade-off. By identifying assets from which you don't require immediate Liquidity, you can place yourself in a position to potentially profit from relatively safe investments that provide a higher than average rate of return.

Choosing Safety and Return over Liquidity can have significant impacts on the accumulation of your assets. In Lawrence's case, the paradigm shift from earning and saving to leveraging assets was a costly one.

> » Lawrence is a corn and soybean farmer with 1,200 acres of land. He routinely retains somewhere between $40,000 and $80,000 in his checking and savings accounts. If a major piece of equipment fails and needs repair or replacement, Lawrence will need the money available to pay for the equipment and carry on with farming. If the price of feed for his cattle goes up one year, he will need to compensate for the increased overhead to his farming operation. He isn't a particularly wealthy farmer, but he has little choice but to keep a portion of money on hand in case something comes up and he must access it quickly. Most of his capital is held in livestock in the pasture or crops in the ground tied up for six to eight months of the year. When a major financial need arises, Lawrence can't just harvest 10 acres of soybeans and use them for payment. He needs to depend heavily on Liquidity in order to be a successful farmer.
>
> Old habits die hard, however, and when Lawrence finally hangs up his overalls and quits farming, he keeps his bank accounts flush with cash, just like in the old days. After selling the farm and the equipment, Lawrence keeps a huge portion of the profits in Liquid investments because that's what he is familiar with. Unfortunately for Lawrence, with his pile of money sitting in his checking account, he isn't even keeping pace with inflation. After all his hard work as a farmer, his money is losing value every day because he didn't shift to a paradigm of leveraging his assets to generate income and accumulate value.
>
> Almost anything would be a better option for Lawrence than clinging to Liquidity. He could have done something

better to get either more return from his money or more safety, and at the very least would not have lost out to inflation.

As you can see, choosing Liquidity solely can be a costly option. The sooner you want your money back, the less you can leverage it for Safety or Return. If you have the option of putting your money in a long-term investment, you will be sacrificing Liquidity, but potentially gaining both Safety and Return.

General confusion often exists about where and when to access your money during retirement. By planning ahead for your cash needs, you can improve your overall returns by employing little-known strategies that can offer you the safety of a bank AND access to your money. These strategies give you the potential to earn higher returns than you would have if the money was sitting in a checking account or under the mattress, as the case may be.

UNCOVERING LITTLE KNOWN STRATEGIES

Most people are familiar with annuities and bonds as long term investments that tie up your money for a given period of time, but there are little-known strategies and products you might not have considered. When used as part of a strategy in an overall plan, these investments can give you greater access to returns and timely liquidity, all while preserving safety. Two options you might ask your financial professional about are mentioned here: the Multi-Year Guaranteed Annuity, known as the MYGA, and the Laddered Bond Strategy.

Let's start with the MYGA:
Multi-Year Guaranteed Annuities are an example of how you can use an annuity as a safe accumulation strategy when you don't need the income right away. Because **these annuities are short-term**—three to five years as opposed to the 10 to 15 year contracts you typically see—you can access your money in a relatively short

period of time. You might even choose to set up several MYGA's using a laddering strategy so that every year, one of your contracts will mature, and you will have access to that lump sum. Meanwhile, the rest of your money is safely growing.

MYGAs offer a set interest rate for a set period of time, so you know exactly how much money you will be earning and when the contract will expire. The MYGA functions very similar to a bank CD, the main difference is they generally offer a more generous rate of return. Who wouldn't want that?

Next, we have the Laddered Bond Strategy:
Bonds can be a confusing investment because although they are sold as a "safe" investment when diversifying a portfolio, we saw earlier how in reality, bonds are a Red Money investment. Just like a stock, bonds go up and down in value, and people take losses. On the day that you buy a bond, it has a market value just like a stock price. This means that on the given day you sell, you will get what the market gives you. There is a better way to use bonds.

As part of an engineered retirement, it is possible to structure the bonds so you hold them until maturity in order to prevent market loss. If you purchase a bond for $100 for example, and then after one year suddenly realize that you need the money, and that bond's market value is now worth $50, then you will be put in the position of having to take a loss. If you wait and hold that bond until full term, then you will get your full $100 back. By purchasing multiple bonds at different time periods, you can give yourself access to your money as the different bonds mature, thus earning you safer returns.

Generally speaking, the interest rates for a 5-year bond will be better than the interest rates offered by a 1-year bond. In order to take advantage of that, we blend and ladder multiple bonds in order to achieve the desired mix of liquidity to fit your needs. As the bonds mature, you can buy another one if the rates are good, or buy a new car if that is what you need. The choice is yours. By employing this laddering strategy, your plan gets an extra layer of flexibility built right in so you continue to have options every year as the economy and circumstances of your life change.

How much Liquidity do you need? Think about it. If you haven't sat down and created an income plan for your retirement, your perceived need for Liquidity is a guess. You don't know how much cash you'll need to fill the income gap if you don't know the amount of your Social Security benefit of the total of your other income options. If you *have* determined your income need and made a plan for filling your income gap, you can partition your assets based on when you will need them. With an income plan in place, ***you can use the three pillars of Liquidity, Safety and Return to enjoy greater returns, access to your cash and peace of mind.***

CHAPTER 8 TAKE-AWAY //

- By being strategic with your cash planning needs, you can still earn returns while having the same level of safety and liquidity you would have if the money was just sitting in the bank.

9
TAX PLANNING DURING RETIREMENT

*"Projects we have completed demonstrate what we know—
future projects decide what we will learn."*
– Dr. Mohsin Tiwana

Taxes play a starring role in the theater of retirement planning. Everyone is familiar with taxes (you've been paying them your entire working life), but not everyone is familiar with how to make tax planning a part of their retirement strategy.

Taxes are taxes, right? You'll pay them before retirement and you'll pay them during retirement. What's the difference? The truth is that a planful approach to taxes can help you save money, protect your assets and ensure that your legacy remains intact.

How can a tax form do all that? The answer lies in planning. **Tax planning** and **tax reporting** are two very different things.

Most people only *report* their taxes. March rolls around, people pull out their 1040s or use TurboTax to enter their income and taxable assets, and ship it off to Uncle Sam at the IRS. If you use a CPA to report your taxes, you are essentially paying them to record history. **You have the option of being proactive with your taxes and to plan for your future by making smart, informed decisions about how taxes affect your overall financial plan.** Working with a financial professional who, along with a CPA, makes recommendations about your finances to you, will keep you looking forward instead of in the rearview mirror as you enter retirement.

FOUR STEPS TO ZERO TAXES DURING RETIREMENT

When you retire, you move from the earning and accumulation phase of your life into the asset distribution phase of your life. For most people, that means relying on Social Security, a 401(k), an IRA, or a pension. Wherever you have put your money for retirement, you are going to start relying on it to provide you with the income that once came as a paycheck.

Step One of our "four steps to zero" process is accepting the facts. Most of your distributions will be considered income by the IRS and will be taxed as such. There are exceptions to that (not all of your Social Security income is taxed, and income from Roth IRAs is not taxed), but for the most part, your distributions will be subject to income taxes.

Step Two is to analyze your individual situation. Just as we can assign colors to describe the risk your money is exposed to, we can also divide your assets into three different buckets of money from a tax standpoint. Those three buckets are:
    1. TAXABLE: The money in this bucket is taxed only on the gains it earns, but you have to pay the tax whether you

spend the money or not. It includes any money you have in your savings, interest-earning checking accounts, bank CDs, and dividend earning stocks.
2. TAX-DEFERRED: The money in this bucket is taxed when you withdraw it, or take it out of the bucket. It should be noted that 100 percent of this money will be taxed, meaning you are taxed on the money in the bucket AND the interest earned. This includes any money you have in a 401(k), 403(b), SEP, IRA, 457 and so forth.
3. TAX-FREE: This is the most desirable bucket of money to have during retirement because the money in this bucket is NOT TAXED. Yipee! It both grows tax-deferred and you don't have to pay taxes when you take the money out of the bucket. Pretty good deal, right? This bucket primarily includes money in Roth IRAs, some cash-value life insurance policies, and depending on your other income, potentially Social Security income.

We talked earlier how Social Security income was originally set up to be a tax-free source of income for retirees, however, that ship has sailed (step one—accept the facts) and now, you can't really put Social Security in the tax-free bucket. You might call it "tax-preferred" because the taxable amount will be anywhere from zero percent to 85 percent, depending on the combined total of your other income during retirement.* So, putting Social Security aside for the moment, ask yourself, if you knew that taxes were going UP by 10, 20 or even 50 percent sometime during the next 20 years, which bucket are you most concerned about?

Step Three is to arrange your optimal account buckets. If all the money you are saving for retirement goes into your 401(k),

---

* *https://www.ssa.gov/planners/taxes.html*

it grows tax deferred. While this is a great way to save, when it comes time to take that money out for income, what you have is essentially a big bucket of taxable money. Your tax rate might be 35 percent today, but there is a very real possibility that rate could be much higher tomorrow.

You do have the opportunity to shift or move your buckets of money around during different stages of your life to use tax law to your advantage. What is the proper amount of money to have in each bucket? The answer depends on your specific situation, but generally speaking, from a tax perspective, the following list gives you a good target to strive for:

1. BUCKET #1: Six months' worth of income needs. You might think of this as your emergency account or your cash reserves. This is money you can access quickly and easily, and if you don't need to use it, the interest it earns is relatively low, so the taxes you pay aren't too high.

2. BUCKET #2: As little as possible. Your strategy for achieving this will depend on your other non-Social Security income sources. When you engineer a retirement, you can literally *earn more money by saving money* on the amount of taxers you pay. In many cases, you can use tax law to your advantage by choosing different investments that can still achieve your goals while lightening your tax burden.

3. BUCKET #3: As much as possible. To shift your assets from the first two buckets into bucket number three requires ingenuity, creativity and the guidance of a professional. Tax-free options such as Roth IRA contributions, Roth IRA conversions (see Chapter 11) and life insurance retirement plans can work in your favor if you know how to use tax law to your advantage.

Step #4: Act now before it's too late. Your specific action plan will depend on many factors, including your age, health, current tax buckets, income sources and you retirement goals. In general, the goal is to ultimately moves as much money as possible into bucket number three so you never have to pay Uncle Sam another penny in retirement. If you feel taxes will likely be going up in the future, then now is the time to implement a plan. Working with an independent financial professional who has experience structuring comprehensive retirement income plans can help you move toward the goal of ZERO taxes throughout retirement.

THE RMD FACTOR: FUTURE INCOME PLANNING

Regarding assets that you have in an IRA or a 401(k) plan that uses an IRA, when you reach 70 ½ years of age, you will be required to draw a certain amount of money from your IRA as income each year. That amount depends on your age and the balance in your IRA. The amount that you are required to withdraw as income is called a Required Minimum Distribution (RMD). Why are you required to withdraw money from your own account? Chances are the money in that account has grown over time, and the government wants to collect taxes on that growth. If you have a large balance in an IRA, there's a chance your RMD could increase your income significantly enough to put you into a higher tax bracket, subjecting you to a higher tax rate.

Here's where tax planning can really begin to work strongly in your favor. In the distribution phase of your life, you have a predictable income based on your RMDs, your Social Security benefit and any other income-generating assets you may have. What really impacts you at this stage is how much of that money you keep in your pocket after taxes. When people decide to leverage the experience and resources of a financial professional, they may not be thinking of how distribution planning and tax planning will benefit their portfolios. Often more exciting prospects like planning income annuities, investing in the market and structuring investments for growth rule the day. Taxes, however, play a crucial role in retirement planning. Achieving those tax goals requires knowledge of options, foresight and professional guidance.

Finding the path to a good tax plan isn't always a simple task. Every tax return you file is different from the one before it because things constantly change. Your expenses change. Planned or unplanned purchases occur. Health care costs, medical bills, an inheritance, property purchases, reaching an age where your RMD kicks in or travel, any number of things can affect how much income you report and how many deductions you take each year.

Preparing for the ever-changing landscape of your financial life requires a tax-diversified portfolio that can be leveraged to balance the incomes, expenditures and deductions that affect you each year. A financial professional will work with you to answer questions like these:

- What does your tax landscape look like?
- Do you have a tax-diversified portfolio robust enough to adapt to your needs?
- Do you have a diversity of taxable and non-taxable income planned for your retirement?
- Will you be able to maximize your distributions to take advantage of your deductions when you retire?
- Is your portfolio strong enough and tax-diversified enough to adapt to an ever-changing (and usually increasing) tax code?

» When Doris returns home after a week in the hospital recovering from a knee replacement, the 77-year-old calls her daughter, sister and brother to let them know she is home and feeling well. She also should have called her CPA. Doris's medical expenses for the procedure, her hospital stay, her

medications and the ongoing physical therapy she attended amount to more than $50,000.

Americans can deduct medical expenses that are more than 10 percent of their Adjusted Gross Income (AGI). Doris's AGI is $60,000 the year of her knee replacement, meaning she is able to deduct $45,500 of her medical bills from her taxes that year.* Her AGI dictated that she could deduct more than 80 percent of her medical expenses that year. **Doris didn't know this.**

Had she been working with a financial professional who regularly asked her about any changes in her life, her spending, or her expenses (expected or unexpected), Doris could have saved thousands of dollars. Doris can also file an amendment to her tax return to recoup the overpayment.

This relatively simple example of how tax planning can save you money is just the tip of the iceberg. No one can be expected to know the entire U.S. tax code. But a professional who is working with a team of CPAs and financial professionals have an advantage over the average taxpayer who must start from square one on their own every year. Have you been taking advantage of all the deductions that are available to you? Remember, during retirement, *you* **will make more money saving on taxes than you will by making more money.**

PROACTIVE TAX PLANNING

The implications of proactive tax planning are far reaching, and are larger than many people realize. Remember, doing your taxes in January, February, March or April means you are writing a history book. Planning your taxes in October, November or December means that you are writing the story as it happens. You can look at

---

* *This scenario presumes permanent laws in effect subsequent to 12/31/16*

all the factors that are at play and make decisions that will impact your tax return *before* you file it.

Realizing that tax planning is an aspect of financial planning is an important leap to make. When you incorporate tax planning into your financial planning strategy, it becomes part of the way you maximize your financial potential. Paying less in taxes means you keep more of your money. Simply put, the more money you keep, the more of it you can leverage as an asset. This kind of planning can affect you at any stage of your life. If you are 40 years old, are you contributing the maximum amount to your 401(k) plan? Are you contributing to a Roth IRA? Are you finding ways to structure the savings you are dedicating to your children's education? Do you have life insurance? Taxes and tax planning affects all of these investment tools. Having a relationship with a professional who works with a CPA can help you build a truly comprehensive financial plan that not only works with your investments, but also shapes your assets to find the most efficient ways to prepare for tax time. There may be years that you could benefit from higher distributions because of the tax bracket that you are in, or there could be years you would benefit from taking less. There may be years when you have a lot of deductions and years you have relatively few. **Adapting your distributions to work in concert with your available deductions** is at the heart of smart tax planning. Professional guidance can bring you to the next level of income distribution, allowing you to remain flexible enough to maximize your tax efficiency. And remember, saving money on taxes makes you more money than making money does.

What you have on paper is important: your assets, savings, investments, which are financial expression of your work and time. It's just as important to know how to get it off the paper in a way that keeps most of it in your pocket. Almost anything that involves financial planning also involves taxes. Annuities, investments, IRAs, 401(k)s, 403(b), and many other investment options will have tax implications. Life also has a way of throwing curveballs. Illness, expensive car repair or replacement, or *any event that has a financial impact on your life will likely have a corresponding tax implication* around which you should adapt your financial plan. Tax planning does just that.

One dollar can end up being less than 25 cents to your heirs.

> » When Mark's father passed away, he discovered that he was the beneficiary of his father's $500,000 IRA. Mark has a wife and a family of four children, and he knew that his father had intended for a large portion of the IRA to go toward funding their college educations.
>
> After Mark's father's estate is distributed, Mark, who is 50 years old and whose two oldest sons are entering college, liquidates the IRA. By doing so, his taxable income for that year puts him in a 39.6 percent tax bracket, immediately reducing the value of the asset to $302,000. An additional 3.8 percent surtax on net investment income further diminishes the funds to $283,000. Liquidating the IRA in effect subjects much of Mark's regular income to the surtax, as well. At this point, Mark will be taxed at 43.4 percent.
>
> Mark's state taxes are an additional 9 percent. Moreover, estate taxes on Mark's father's assets claim another 22 percent. By the time the IRS is through, Mark's income from the IRA will be taxed at 75 percent, leaving him with $125,000 of the original $500,000. While it would help contribute to the education of his children, it wouldn't come anywhere near completely paying for it, something the $500,000 could have easily done.

As the above example makes clear, leaving an asset to your beneficiaries can be more complicated than it may seem. In the case of a traditional IRA, after federal, estate and state taxes, the asset could literally diminish to as little as 25 percent of its value.

How does working with a professional help you make smarter tax decisions with your own finances? Any financial professional worth their salt will be working with a firm that has a team of trained tax professionals, including CPAs, who have an intimate knowledge of the tax code and how to adapt a financial plan to it.

Here's another example of how taxes have major implications on asset management:

> » *Bob and Catherine, a 62-year-old couple, begin working with a financial professional in October. After structuring their assets to reflect their risk tolerance and creating assets that would provide them Green Money income during retirement, they feel good about their situation. They make decisions that allow them to maximize their Social Security benefits, they have plenty of options for filling their income gap, and have begun a safe yet ambitious Yellow Money strategy with their professional. When their professional asks them about their tax plan, they tell him their CPA handled their taxes every year, and did a great job. Their professional says, "I don't mean who does your taxes, I mean, who does your tax planning?" Bob and Catherine aren't sure how to respond.*
>
> *Their professional brings Bob and Catherine's financial plan to the firm's CPA and has her run a tax projection for them. A week later their professional calls them with a tax plan for the year that will save them more than $3,000 on their tax return. The couple is shocked. A simple piece of advice from the CPA based on the numbers revealed that if they paid their estimated taxes before the end of the year, they would be able to itemize it as a deduction, allowing them to save thousands of dollars.*

This solution won't work for everyone, and it may not work for Bob and Catherine every year. That's not the point. By being proactive with their approach to taxes and using the resources made available by their financial professional, they were able to create a tax plan that saved them money.

YELLOW MONEY AND TAXES

There are also tax implications for the money that you have managed professionally. People with portions of their investment portfolio that are actively traded can particularly benefit from having a proactive tax strategy. Without going into too much detail, for tax purposes there are two kinds of investment money: qualified and non-qualified. Different investment strategies can have different effects on how you are taxed on your investments and the growth of your investments. Some are more beneficial for one kind of investment strategy over another. Determining how to plan for the taxation of non-qualified and qualified investments is fodder for holiday party discussions at accounting firms. While it may not be a stimulating topic for the average investor, you don't have to understand exactly how it works in order to benefit from it.

While there are many differences between qualified and non-qualified investments, the main difference is this: qualified plans are designed to give investors tax benefits by deferring taxation of their growth until they are withdrawn. Non-qualified investments are not eligible for these deferral benefits. As such, non-qualified investments are taxed whenever income is realized from them in the form of growth.

Actively and non-actively traded investments provide a simple example of how to position your investments for the best tax advantage. In an actively traded and managed portfolio, there is a high amount of buying and selling of stocks, bonds, funds, ETFs, etc. If that active portfolio of non-qualified investments does well and makes a 20 percent return one year and you are in the 39.6 percent tax bracket, your net gain from that portfolio is only about 12 percent (39.6 percent tax of the 20 percent gain is roughly 8 percent.) In a passive trading strategy, you can use a qualified investment tool, such as an IRA, to achieve 13, 14 or 15 percent growth (much lower than the actively traded portfolio), but still realize a higher net return because the growth of the qualified investment is not taxed until it is withdrawn.

Does this mean that you have to always rely on a buy and hold strategy in qualified investment tools? Not necessarily. The question is, if you have qualified and non-qualified investments, where do you want to position your actively traded and managed assets? Incorporating a planful approach to positioning your investments for more beneficial taxation can be done many ways, but let's consider one example. Keeping your actively managed investment strategies inside an IRA or some other qualified plan could allow you to realize the higher gains of those investments without paying tax on their growth every year. Your more passively managed funds could then be kept in taxable, non-qualified vehicles and methods, and because you aren't realizing income from them on an annual basis by frequently trading them, they grow sheltered from taxation.

If you are interested in taking advantage of tax strategies that maximize your net income, you need the attentive strategies, experience and knowledge of a professional who can give you options that position you for profit. At the end of the day, what's important to you as the consumer is how much you keep, your after-tax take home.

ESTATE TAXES

The government doesn't just tax your income from investments while you're alive. They will also dip into your legacy.

While estate taxes aren't as hot of a topic as they were a few years ago, they are still an issue of concern for many people with assets. While taxes may not apply on estates that are less than $5 million, certain states have estate taxes with much lower exclusion ratios. Some are as low as $600,000. Many people may have to pay a state estate tax. One strategy for avoiding those types of taxes is to move assets outside of your estate. That can include gifting them to family or friends, or putting them into an irrevocable trust. Life insurance is another option for protecting your legacy.

CHAPTER 9 TAKE-AWAY //

- If you diversify your taxes just as you would diversify your assets, you can prepare for lower or no taxes during retirement.

10
THE FUTURE OF U.S. TAXATION

"All we know about the new economic world tells us that nations which train engineers will prevail over those which train lawyers. No nation has ever sued its way to greatness."
– Richard Lamm

Although the phrase "nothing is certain except for death and taxes" is most famously attributed to Benjamin Franklin, variations of this saying existed even before the country's first taxes were levied, and these words continue to ring true to this day. However, due to recent upheavals in the American financial landscape, this saying might need to be modified to, "nothing is certain except for death and *increasing* taxes."

Since 2007, the federal debt held by the public has more than doubled relative to the size of the U.S. economy*. With the wellbeing of the economy in jeopardy, legislation regarding debt reduction and tax reform has become a hot button issue. Regardless of what legislation has been, or will be, thrown at the American public, the truth of the matter remains the same: the country's current tax revenues cannot cover its obligations.

If the government wants to keep the lights on, it's going to need more income, which not only means that you can count on being taxed, but also on being taxed at an increasing rate.

DEBT CEILING – CAUSE AND EFFECTS

Since 2000, Congress has raised the debt ceiling more than a dozen times. Increasing the debt ceiling is needed because the government keeps maxing out its credit limit, which it has been reliant upon since the beginning of the Industrial Revolution. Essentially, each time the federal government reaches the end of its line of credit; Congress raises the debt ceiling to extend it. This type of poor money management behavior is nothing new for many Americans: many people overuse their credit cards and rack up an impressive amount of debt. However, most people do not have the ability to raise the credit limit on a card once they have maxed it out—unless they can show they have the ability to pay the balance back. The only way to pay a credit line back is by making more money than you're spending. In other words, responsibility and a balanced budget are critical components to repaying a debt.

The federal government keeps finding ways to increase its credit line without also finding ways to proportionally cut its spending. Although some spending cuts have been put in place, they are not large enough to be worthy adversaries of the current

---

* *https://www.cbo.gov/publication/52142*

debt situation. Consequently, the continual increasing of the debt ceiling has raised more than just the ability of the federal government to go further into debt; it has also raised concerns and fears about the direction in which the economy is heading. As investors' worry about the impact that future investment valuations may have on their personal wealth grows progressively serious, the market continues to swing unpredictably.

The truth of the matter is that raising the debt ceiling is only one part of the equation required to address the country's debt problem—tax reform is the other. If the government wants to try to staunch the flow of its ever-rising debt, then it will need to make more money, and the only way the government makes money is by collecting taxes. Unfortunately, however, the government frequently collects less than it spends: the Congressional Budget Office (CBO) estimated the 2017 budget deficit would be $559 billion*.

DEBT AND EARNINGS

Currently, the national debt is increasing at an unprecedented rate, rising to levels never seen before and threatening serious harm to the economy. In October 2004, the national debt was $7.4 trillion**, and by April 2017 it had climbed to nearly $20 trillion***, which means the national debt grew 270.3 percent during this time period. To further understand the gravity of this situation, consider that economists believe that a sustainable economy's debt exists at a maximum level of approximately 80 percent. In 2014,

---

* *https://www.cbo.gov/publication/52370*
** *CBO, An Update to the Budget and Economic Outlook: 2014 - 2024*
*** *US Department of the Treasury's Bureau of the Fiscal Service, www.treasurydirect.gov/NP/debt/current*

the U.S. national debt was 101.8 percent of the GDP*. By 2017, the U.S. national debt has risen to 104.3 percent of the GDP**.

The significance of these two numbers lies within the contrast. The national debt is the amount that needs to be repaid; this can be thought of as the government's credit card balance. The GDP represents the market value of all goods and services produced within a country during a given period. In other words, the GDP represents the gross taxable income available to the government. If debts are increasing at a rate greater than the gross income available for taxation, then the only way to make up the difference is to increase the rate at which the gross income is being taxed.

Even more concerning is that the disparity between growth in national debt and growth in GDP is projected to continue, which means the amount of money the federal government owes will far outpace its ability to repay it. As anyone who has struggled with debt can tell you, continually borrowing more money than you make can have potentially disastrous consequences.

Unfortunately, analysis of the federal government's budget also shows that regardless of revenue collection rates and increased taxes, the deficit will most likely continue to increase, and without additional spending cuts to help bring the budget into balance, tax increases are likely to continue.

THE END OF AN ERA

From a historical point of view, taxes are extremely low. The last time the U.S. national debt was even close to the same percentage level of GDP as it is today was for several years after the end of World War II. The maximum tax rate at that point, and through the years from 1944 through 1963, averaged 90 percent. Compare

---

* *Federal Reserve Bank of St Louis Economic Research*
** *Federal Reserve Bank of St Louis Economic Research, https://fred.stlouisfed.org/series/ GFDEGDQ188S*

that to the maximum rate of 39.6 percent today, and it becomes very clear that there is a disparity of extreme proportion.

Taxes during this historical period were at extreme levels for nearly 20 years, throughout and following this level of debt-to-GDP. A significant point to note about the difference at that time versus where we are today is the economic activity. The period of 1944 through 1963 was in the heart of both the Industrial Revolution and the birth of the baby-boom generation. Today, we are mired in extreme volatility with frequent periods of boom and bust accompanied by the beginning of the greatest retirement wave ever experienced within the U.S. economy.

To contrast these two time periods with respect to the recovery period is almost asinine, as the external pressures from globalization and domestic unfunded liabilities did not exist or were irrelevant factors during the prior period.

To add insult to injury, U.S. domestic unfunded liabilities were estimated to be about $84 trillion in 2012 and that number has only increased through the intervening years*. These liabilities exist outside of the annual budgetary debt discussed above and are due to items such as Social Security, Medicare and government pensions. The most concerning part of this stems from the fact that we are on the cusp of the greatest retirement wave in U.S. history as the baby-boom generation begins retiring and drawing from the unfunded Social Security for which they currently have entitlement. Over the long-run, expenditures related to healthcare programs such as Medicare and Medicaid are projected to grow faster than the economy overall as the population matures.

To put unfunded liabilities into perspective, consider these as off-balance-sheet obligations similar to those of Enron. Although these are not listed as part of the national debt, they must be

---

* *National Center for Policy Analysis, How Much Does the Federal Government Owe?, June 2012*

paid just the same. The difference between Enron and the U.S. unfunded liabilities is that if the U.S. government cannot come up with the funds to pay all these liabilities through revenue generation then they will print the money necessary to pay the debt.

WHAT DOES THE SOLUTION LOOK LIKE?
Unfortunately, the general public is in a no-win situation for this solution to the problem. Printing money does not bode well for economic growth as this action creates inflationary pressures that devalue the U.S. dollar and make everyone less wealthy. Cutting the entitlements that compose this liability leaves millions of people without benefits they have come to expect. The only other option, and one that the government knows all too well, is increased taxes. In fact, according to a Congressional Budget Office paper issued in 2004*, unfunded liabilities are addressed as follows:

"The term 'unfunded liability' has been used to refer to a gap between the government's projected financial commitment under a particular program and the revenues that are expected to be available to fund that commitment. But no government obligation can be truly considered 'unfunded' because of the U.S. government's sovereign power to tax—which is the ultimate resource to meet its obligations."

A balanced budget is going to be required at some point and with this will come higher taxes. Given our current position and projected budgets, it is likely that tax increases are coming in the near future. However, although raising taxes is a strategy to raise money, it is not a solution to the government's current and pending fiscal problems.

How do you prepare? Why spend so much time reassuring you that taxes will increase? Because you have an opportunity to

---

* CBO paper, *Measures of the U.S. Government's Fiscal Position Under Current Law*, Sept. 2004

take action. Now is the time to prepare for what is to come by structuring countermeasures for the good, the bad, and the ugly of each of these legislative nightmares through tax-advantaged retirement planning.

The truth of the matter is that you make more money by saving on taxes than you do by making more money. The simplistic logic of this statement makes sense when you discover it takes a $1.50 in earnings to put that same dollar, saved in taxes, back in your pocket*. This simple concept becomes extremely valuable to people in retirement and those living on fixed incomes.

As simple as it sounds, it is much more difficult to execute. Most people fail to put together a plan as they near retirement, beginning with a simple cash flow budget. If you have not analyzed your proposed income streams and expenses, you could not possibly have taken the time to position these cash flows and other events into a tax-preferred plan.

Most people will state, "I have a plan" and thus, they do not need any further assistance in this area. The truth in most instances is that many of these people could not show you their plan, and of the few that could, they would not be able to show you how they have executed it. In this regard, they may as well be Richard Nixon saying, "I am not a crook" for as much as they claim, "I have a plan." The truth lies in waiting.

As you approach or begin retirement, you should look at what cash flows you will have. Do you have a pension? How about Social Security? How much additional cash flow are you going to need to draw from your assets to maintain the lifestyle that you desire?

Most people spend their whole lives saving and accumulating wealth but very little time determining a strategy that will distribute this accumulation in ways that will help them to retain it.

Assuming a 33 percent effective tax rate

You need to make sure you have the appropriate diversification of taxable versus non-taxable assets to complement your distribution strategy.

THE BENEFITS OF DIVERSIFICATION

Heading into retirement, you should be situated within a diversified tax landscape. The point to spending your whole life accumulating wealth is not to see how big the number is on paper, but rather to be an exercise in how much you put in your pocket after removing it from the paper.

To truly understand tax diversification, you must understand what types of money exist and how each of these will be treated during accumulation and, most importantly, during distribution. The following is a brief summary:

1. Free money
2. Tax-advantaged money
3. Tax-deferred money
4. Taxable money
    a. Ordinary income
    b. Capital gains and qualified dividends

FREE MONEY

Free money is the best kind of money regardless of the tax treatment, because in the end you have more money than you would have otherwise. Many employers will provide contributions toward employee retirement accounts to offer additional employment benefits and inspire employees to save for their own retirement. With this, employers often will offer a matching contribution in which they will contribute up to a certain percentage of an employee's salary, generally three to five percent, to that employee's retirement account when the employee contributes to their retirement account as well. For example, if an employee earns $50,000 annually and contributes three percent ($1,500) to their retirement account annually, the employer will also contribute three percent ($1,500) to the employee's account. That is $1,500 in free money. Take all that you can get!

TAX-ADVANTAGED MONEY

Tax-advantaged money is the next best thing to free-money. Although you have to earn tax-advantaged money you do not have to give part of it away to Uncle Sam. Tax-advantaged money comes in three basic forms that you can utilize during your lifetime; four if prison inspires your future, but it's not necessary to discuss that option.

One of the most commonly known forms of tax-advantaged money is municipal bonds, which earn and pay interest that could be federally tax-advantaged, state tax-advantaged, or both state and federal tax-advantaged. There are several caveats that should be discussed in regard to the notion of tax-advantaged income from municipal bonds. First, you will notice that tax-advantaged has several flavors from the state and federal perspective. This is because states will generally tax the interest earned on a municipal bond unless the bond is offered from an entity located within that state. This severely limits the availability of completely tax-advantaged municipal bonds and constrains underlying risk and liquidity factors. Second, municipal bond interest gets added back into the equation for determining your modified adjusted gross income (MAGI) for Social Security and could push your income above the thresholds subjecting a portion of your Social Security income to taxation. In effect, if this interest subjects some other income to taxation then this interest is truly being taxed. Last, municipal bond interest may be excluded from the regular federal tax system, but it is included for determining tax under the alternative minimum tax (AMT) system. In its basic form, the AMT system is a separate tax system that applies if the tax computed under AMT exceeds the tax computed under the regular tax system, the difference between these two computations is the alternative minimum tax.

TAX-FREE MONEY: ROTH IRA

Roth accounts are probably the single greatest tax asset that has come from Congress outside of life insurance and are well known but rarely used. Roth IRAs were first established by the Taxpayer Relief Act of 1997 and were named after Senator William Roth, the chief sponsor of the legislation. A Roth account is simply an account in the form of an IRA or an employer-sponsored retirement account that allows for tax-advantaged growth of earnings and, thus, tax-advantaged income.

The main difference between a Roth and a traditional IRA or employer-sponsored plan lies within the timing of the taxation. You're probably very familiar with the typical scenario of putting money away for retirement through an employer plan, whereby your employer deducts money from each paycheck and puts it directly into a retirement account. This money is taken out before taxes are calculated meaning you do not pay tax on those earnings today. A Roth account, on the other hand, takes the money *after* the taxes have been taken out and then puts it into the retirement account, so you do pay tax on the money today. The other significant difference between these two is taxation during distribution in later years. With a traditional retirement account, when you take the money out later it gets added to your ordinary income and is taxed accordingly. Additionally, including this in your income subjects you to the consequences previously mentioned for municipal bonds with Social Security taxation, AMT, as well as higher Medicare premiums. A Roth, on the other hand, has tax-advantaged distributions and does not contribute toward negative impact items such as Social Security taxation, AMT, or Medicare premium increases. It essentially comes back to you without tax and other obligations.

The best way to consider the difference between the two accounts is to look at the life of a farmer. A farmer will buy seed, plant it in the ground, grow the crops, and harvest it later for sale. Typically, the farmer would only pay tax on the crops that have been harvested and sold. But if you were the farmer, would you rather pay tax on $5,000 worth of seed that you plant today or $50,000 worth of harvested crop later? The obvious answer is $5,000 worth of seed today. The truth of the matter is that you are a farmer, except you are planting dollars into your retirement account instead of seeds into the earth.

So why doesn't everyone have a Roth retirement account if things are so simple? There are several reasons, but the single greatest reason has been the constraints on contributions. If you earned over certain thresholds (MAGI over $133,000 single and $196,000 joint for 2017), you were not eligible to make contributions, and, until 2010, if your modified adjusted gross income (MAGI) was over $100,000 (single or joint) then you could not convert a traditional IRA to a Roth. Outside of these contribution limits, most people save for retirement through their employers and most employers are not offering Roth options within their plans. The reason behind this is because Roth accounts are not that well understood and people have been educated to believe that saving on taxes today is the best possible course of action.

TAX-FREE MONEY: LIFE INSURANCE

As previously mentioned, the single greatest tax asset that has come from Congress outside of life insurance is the Roth account. Life insurance is the little known or discussed tax asset that holds some of the greatest value for your financial history both during life and upon death, and it is by far the best tax-advantaged device available. Traditionally, life insurance is viewed as a way to protect your loved ones from financial ruin upon your demise and it should be noted that everyone who cares about someone should have life insurance. By purchasing a life insurance policy, your loved ones will be assured a financial windfall from the life insurance company when you die that will help them with your final expenses and carry on their lives without you comfortably. The best part about the life insurance windfall is the fact that nobody will have to pay tax on the money received. This is the single greatest tax-advantaged device available, but it has one downside, you do not get to use it. Only your heirs will.

The little known and discussed part of life insurance is the cash value build-up within whole life and universal life (permanent) policies. Life insurance is not typically seen as an investment vehicle for building wealth and retirement planning, although it should briefly be discussed why this thought process should be re-evaluated. Permanent life insurance is generally misconceived as something that is very expensive for a wealth accumulation vehicle as there are mortality charges (fees for the death benefit) that detract from the returns that are available and further, those returns do not yield as much as the stock market over the long run. This is why many times you will hear the phrase "buy term and invest the rest," where "term" refers to term insurance.

It's important to review the two terms just used in regard to life insurance: term and permanent. Term insurance is what most people are familiar with. You purchase a certain death benefit that will go to your heirs upon your death and this policy will be in effect for a certain number of years, typically 10 to 20 years. The 10 to 20 years is the term of the policy and once you have reached that end you no longer have insurance unless you purchase another policy at that point.

On the other hand, permanent insurance has no term involved, it is permanent as long as the premiums continue to be paid. Permanent insurance generally has higher premiums than term insurance for the same amount of death benefit coverage and it is this difference that is referred to when people say "invest the rest."

Simply speaking, there are significant differences between these two policies that do not get taken into consideration when providing a comparative analysis in the numbers. One item that gets lost in the fray when comparing term and permanent insurance is that term usually expires before death, in fact insurance studies show less than 1 percent of all term policies pay out death benefit claims. The issue arises when the term expires and the desire to have more insurance is still present. A term policy with the same benefit will be much more expensive than the original policy and, many times, life events occur, such as cancer or heart conditions, which makes it impossible to acquire another policy and leaves your loved ones unprotected and tax-advantaged legacy planning out of the equation.

Another aspect and probably the most important piece in consideration of the future of taxation is the fact that permanent insurance has a cash accumulation value. Two aspects stand out with the cash accumulation value. First, as the cash accumulation value increases the death benefit will also increase whereas term insurance is level. Second, this cash accumulation offers value to you during your lifetime rather than just your heirs upon death. The cash accumulation value can be used for tax-advantaged income during your lifetime through policy loans. Most importantly, this tax-advantaged income is available during retirement for distribution planning, all while offering the same typical financial protection to your heirs.

TAX-DEFERRED MONEY

Tax-deferred money is the type of money from which most people are familiar, but the idea was also briefly reviewed above. Tax-deferred money is typically your traditional IRA, employer sponsored retirement plan, or a non-qualified annuity. Essentially, money is put into an investment vehicle that will accumulate in value over time and you do not pay taxes on the earnings that grow in these accounts until it is distributed. Taxes must be paid once the money is distributed and, in addition to the taxes, the same negative consequences exist toward additional taxation and expense in other areas as previously discussed.

TAXABLE MONEY

Taxable money is everything else and is taxable both today and later, whenever it is received.

Of these four types of money, they really come down to two distinct classifications: taxable and tax-advantaged.

The greatest difference when comparing taxable and tax-advantaged income is a function of how much money you will keep after tax. For help in determining what the differences should be, excluding outside factors such as Social Security taxation and AMT, a tax equivalent yield should be used.

TAX-FREE IN THE REAL WORLD

To put the tax equivalent yield into perspective, consider the following example:

> » *Bob and Mary are currently retired and in the 25 percent tax bracket living on Social Security and interest from investments. They have a substantial portion of their investments in municipal bonds yielding 6 percent, which in today's market is quite comforting. The tax equivalent yield they would need to earn from a taxable investment would be 8 percent, a 2 percent gap which seems almost impossible given current market volatility. However, something that has never been put into perspective is that the interest from their municipal bonds is subject to taxation on their Social Security benefits (at 21.25 percent). With this, the yield on their municipal bonds would be 4.725 percent, and the taxable equivalent yield falls to 6.3 percent leaving a gap of only 1.575 percent.*

In the end, most people spend their lives accumulating wealth through the best, if not only vehicle they know, a tax-deferred account. This account is most likely a 401(k) or 403(b) plan offered through your employer and may be supplemented with an IRA that was established at one point or another. As the years go by, people blindly throw money into these accounts in an effort to save for a retirement that they someday hope to reach.

The truth is most people have an age selected for when they would like to retire but spend their lives wondering if they will ever be able to actually quit working. To answer this question, you must understand how much money you will have available to contribute toward your needs. In other words, you need to know what your after-tax income will be during this period.

All else being equal, it would not matter if you put your money into a taxable, tax-deferred, or tax-advantaged account as long as income tax rates never change and outside factors are never an event. The net amount you receive in the end will be the same. Unfortunately, this will never be the case. We already know that taxes will increase in the future, meaning we will likely see higher taxes in retirement than during our peak earning years.

Regardless, saving for retirement in any form is a good thing since it appears from all practical perspectives that future government benefits will be cut and taxes will increase. You have the ability to plan today for efficient tax diversification and maximization of your after-tax dollars during your distribution years.

CHAPTER 10 TAKE-AWAY //
- You make more money by saving on taxes than you do by making more money. This simple concept becomes extremely valuable to people in retirement and those living on fixed incomes.

11
THE FUTURE OF YOUR TAXATION

"Anything which is physically possible can always be made financially possible; money is the bugaboo of small minds."
– Robert A. Heinlein

Louis Brandeis provides one of the best examples illustrating how tax planning works. Brandeis was Associate Justice on the Supreme Court of the United States from 1916 to 1939. Born in Louisville, Kentucky, Brandeis was an intelligent man with a touch of country charm. He described tax planning this way:

"I live in Alexandria, Virginia. Near the Court Chambers, there is a toll bridge across the Potomac. When in a rush, I pay the dollar toll and get home early. However, I usually drive outside the downtown section of the city and cross the Potomac on a free bridge.

The bridge was placed outside the downtown Washington, D.C. area to serve a useful social service—getting drivers to drive the extra mile and help alleviate congestion during the rush hour.

If I went over the toll bridge and through the barrier without paying a toll, I would be committing tax evasion.

If I drive the extra mile and drive outside the city of Washington to the free bridge, I am using a legitimate, logical and suitable method of tax avoidance, and I am performing a useful social service by doing so.

*The tragedy is that **few people know that the free bridge exists.**"*

Like Brandeis, most American taxpayers have options when it comes to "crossing the Potomac," so to speak. It's a financial planner's job to tell you what options are available. You can wait until March to file your taxes, at which time you might pay someone to report and pay the government a larger portion of your income. However, you could instead file before the end of the year, work with your financial professional and incorporate a tax plan as part of your overall financial planning strategy. Filing later is like crossing the toll bridge. Tax planning is like crossing the free bridge.

Which would you rather do?

The answer to this question is easy. **Most people want to save money and pay less in taxes.** What makes this situation really difficult in real life, however, is that the signs along the side of the road that direct us to the free bridge are not that clear. To normal Americans, and to plenty of people who have studied it, the U.S. tax code is easy to get lost in. There are all kinds of rules, exceptions to rules, caveats and conditions that are difficult to understand, or even to know about. What you really need to know is your options and the bottom line impacts of those options.

ROTH IRA CONVERSIONS

The attractive qualities of Roth IRAs may have prompted you to explore the possibility of moving some of your assets into a Roth account. Another important difference between the accounts is how they treat Required Minimum Distributions (RMDs). When you turn 70 ½ years old, you are required to take a minimum amount of money out of a traditional IRA. This amount is your RMD. It is treated as taxable income. Roth IRAs, however, do not have RMDs, and their distributions are not taxable. Quite a deal, right?

While having a Roth IRA as part of your portfolio is a good idea, converting assets to a Roth IRA can pose some challenges, depending on what kinds of assets you want to transfer.

One common option is the conversion of a traditional IRA to a Roth IRA. You may have heard about converting your IRA to a Roth IRA, but you might not know the full net result on your income. The main difference between the two accounts is that the growth of investments within a traditional IRA is not taxed until income is withdrawn from the account, whereas taxes are charged on contribution amounts to a Roth IRA, not withdrawals. The problem, however, is that when assets are removed from a traditional IRA, even if the assets are being transferred to a Roth IRA account, taxes apply.

There are a lot of reasons to look at Roth conversions. People have a lot of money in IRAs, up to multiple millions of dollars. Even with $500,000, when they turn 70 ½ years old, their RMD is going to be approximately $18,000, and they have to take that out whether they want to or not. It's a tax issue. Essentially, if you will be subject to high RMDs, it could have impacts on how much of your Social Security is taxable, and on your tax bracket.

By paying taxes now instead of later on assets in a Roth IRA, you can realize tax-advantaged growth. You pay once and you're done paying. Your heirs are done paying. It's a powerful tool. Here's a simple example to show you how powerful it can be:

Imagine that you pay to convert a traditional IRA to a Roth. You have decided that you want to put the money in a vehicle that gives you a tax-advantaged income option down the road. If you pay a 25 percent tax on that conversion and the Roth IRA then doubles in value over the next 10 years, you could look at your situation as only having paid 12.5 percent tax.

The prospect of tax-advantaged income is a tempting one. While you have to pay a conversion tax to transfer your assets, you also have turned taxable income into tax free retirement money that you can let grow as long as you want without being required to withdraw it.

There are options, however, that address this problem. Much like the Brandeis story, there may be a "free bridge" option for many investors.

Your financial professional will likely tell you that it is not a matter of whether or not you should perform a Roth IRA conversion, it is a matter of how much you should convert and when.

Here are some of the things to consider before converting to a Roth IRA:

- If you make a conversion before you retire, you may end up paying higher taxes on the conversion because it is likely that you are in some of your highest earning years, placing you in the highest tax bracket of your life. It is possible that a better strategy would be to wait until after you retire, a time when you may have less taxable income, which would place you in a lower tax bracket.

- Many people opt to reduce their work hours from fulltime to part-time in the years before they retire. If you have pursued this option, your income will likely be lower, in turn lowering your tax rate.

THE FUTURE OF YOUR TAXATION

- The first years that you draw Social Security benefits can also be years of lower reported income, making it another good time frame in which to convert to a Roth IRA.

One key strategy to handling a Roth IRA conversion is to *always be able to pay the cost of the tax conversion with outside money.* Structuring your tax year to include something like a significant deduction can help you offset the conversion tax. This way you aren't forced to take the money you need for taxes from the value of the IRA. The reason taxes apply to this maneuver is because when you withdraw money from a traditional IRA, it is treated as taxable income by the IRS. Your financial professional, with the help of the CPAs at their firm, may be able to provide you with options like after-tax money, itemized deductions or other situations that can pose effective tax avoidance options.

Some examples of avoiding Roth IRA conversions taxes include:

- *Using medical expenses that are above 10 percent of your Adjusted Gross Income.* If you have health care costs that you can list as itemized deductions, you can convert an amount of income from a traditional IRA to a Roth IRA that is offset by the deductible amount. Essentially, deductible medical expenses negate the taxes resulting from recording the conversion.
- *Individuals, usually small business owners, who are dealing with a Net Operating Loss (NOL).* If you have NOLs, but aren't able to utilize all of them on your tax return, you can carry them forward to offset the taxable income from the taxes on income you convert to a Roth IRA.
- *Charitable giving.* If you are charitably inclined, you can use the amount of your donations to reduce the amount of taxable income you have during that year. By matching the amount you convert to a Roth IRA to the amount

your taxable income was reduced by charitable giving, you can essentially avoid taxation on the conversion. You may decide to double your donations to a charity in one year, giving them two years' worth of donations in order to offset the Roth IRA conversion tax on this year's tax return.

- *Investments that are subject to depletion.* Certain investments can kick off depletion expenses. If you make an investment and are subject to depletion expenses, they can be deducted and used to offset a Roth IRA conversion tax.

Not all of the above scenarios work for everyone, and there are many other options for offsetting conversion taxes. The point is that you have options, and your financial professional and tax professional can help you understand those options.

If you have a traditional IRA, Roth conversions are something you should look at. As you approach retirement you should consider your options and make choices that keep more of your money in your pocket, not the government's.

ADDITIONAL TAX BENEFITS OF ROTH IRAS

Not only do Roth IRAs provide you with tax-advantaged growth, they also give you a tax diversified landscape that allows you to maximize your distributions. Chances are that no matter the circumstances, you will have taxed income and other assets subject to taxation. *But if you have a Roth IRA, you have the unique ability to manage your Adjusted Gross Income (AGI), because you have a tax-advantaged income option!*

Converting to a Roth IRA can also help you preserve and build your legacy. Because Roth IRAs are exempt from RMDs, after you make a conversion from a traditional IRA, your Roth account can grow tax-advantaged for another 15, 20 or 25 years and it can be used as tax-advantaged income by your heirs. It is important to note, however, that non-spousal beneficiaries do have to take RMDs from a Roth IRA, or choose to stretch it and draw tax-advantaged income out of it over their lifetime.

TO CONVERT OR NOT TO CONVERT?

Conversions aren't only for retirees. You can convert at any time. Your choice should be based on your individual circumstances and tax situation. Sticking with a traditional IRA or converting to a Roth, again, depends on your individual circumstances, including your income, your tax bracket and the amount of deductions you have each year.

Is it better to have a Roth IRA or traditional IRA? It depends on your individual circumstance. Some people don't mind having taxable income from an IRA. Their income might not be very high and their RMD might not bump their tax bracket up, so it's not as big a deal. A similar situation might involve income from Social Security. Social Security benefits are taxed based on other income you are drawing. If you are in a position where none or very little of your Social Security benefit is subject to taxes, paying income tax on your RMD may be very easy.

> *There are also situations where leveraging taxable income from a traditional IRA can work to your advantage come tax time. For example, Mike and Mollie dream of buying a boat when they retire. It is something they have looked forward to their entire marriage. In addition to the savings and investments that they created to supply them with income during retirement, which includes a traditional IRA, they have also saved money for the sole purpose of purchasing a boat once they stop working.*
>
> *When the time comes and they finally buy the boat of their dreams, they pay an additional $15,000 in sales taxes that year because of the large purchase. Because they are retired*

and earning less money, the deductions they used to be able to realize from their income taxes are no longer there. The high amount of sales taxes they paid on the boat puts them in a position where they could benefit from taking taxable income from a traditional IRA.

When Mike and Mollie's financial professional learns about their purchase, he immediately contacts a CPA at his firm to run the numbers. They determine that by taking a $15,000 distribution from their IRA, they could fulfill their income needs to offset the $15,000 sales tax deduction that they were claiming due to the purchase of their boat. In the end, they pay zero taxes on their income distribution from their IRA.

The moral of the story? **Having a tax diversified landscape gives you options.** Having capital assets that can be liquidated, tax-advantaged income options and sources that can create capital gains or capital losses will put you in a position to play your cards right no matter what you want to accomplish with your taxes. The ace up your sleeve is your financial professional and the CPAs they work with. Do yourself a favor and *plan* your taxes instead of *reporting* them!

CHAPTER 11 TAKE-AWAY //

- There are currently no IRS limits on how much a person can convert from an IRA to a Roth IRA, but this might not be the case five or 10 years from now. By timing a conversion correctly, you can pay taxes now at historically low rates and protect your family from future taxes.

12
YOUR LEGACY BEYOND DOLLARS AND CENTS

"Anyone who keeps learning stays young."
– Henry Ford

If you're like most people, planning your estate isn't on the top of your list of things to do. Planning your income needs for retirement, managing your assets and just living your life without worrying about how your estate will be handled when you are gone make legacy planning less than attractive for a Saturday afternoon task. The fact of the matter, however, is that if you don't plan your legacy, someone else will. That someone else is usually a combination of the IRS and other government entities: lawyers, executors, courts, and accountants. Who do you think has the best interests of your beneficiaries in mind?

Today, there is more consideration given to planning a legacy than just maximizing your estate. When most people think about an estate, it may seem like something only the very wealthy have: a stately manor or an enormous business. But a legacy is something else entirely. A legacy is more than the sum total of the financial assets you have accumulated. It is the lasting impression you make on those you leave behind. The dollar and cents are just a small part of a legacy.

A legacy encompasses the stories that others tell about you, shared experiences and values. An estate may pay for college tuition, but a legacy may inform your grandchildren about the importance of higher education and self-reliance.

A legacy may also contain family heirlooms or items of emotional significance. It may be a piece of art your great-grandmother painted, family photos, or a childhood keepsake.

When you go about planning your legacy, certainly explore strategies that can maximize the financial benefit to the ones you care about. But also take the time to ensure that you have organized the whole of your legacy, and let that be a part of the last gift you leave.

Many people avoid planning their legacy until they feel they must. Something may change in your life, like the birth of a grandchild, the diagnosis of a serious health problem, or the death of a close friend or loved one. Waiting for tragedy to strike in order to get your affairs in order is not the best course of action. The emotional stress of that kind of situation can make it hard to make patient, thoughtful decisions. Taking the time to create a premeditated and thoughtful legacy plan will assure that your assets will be transferred where and when you want them when the time comes.

THE BENEFITS OF PLANNING YOUR LEGACY

The distribution of your assets, whether in the form of property, stocks, Individual Retirement Accounts, 401(k)s or liquid assets, can be a complicated undertaking if you haven't left clear instructions about how you want them handled. Not having a plan will cost more money and take more time, leaving your loved ones to wait (sometimes for years) and receive less of your legacy than if you had a clear plan.

Planning your legacy will help your assets be transferred with little delay and little confusion. Instead of leaving decisions about how to distribute your estate to your family, attorneys or financial professionals, preserve your legacy and your wishes by drafting a clear plan at an early age.

And while you know all that, it can still be hard to sit down and do it. It reminds you that life is short, and the relatively complicated nature of sorting through your assets can feel like a daunting task. But one thing is for sure: *it is impossible for your assets to be transferred or distributed the way you want at the end of your life if you don't have a plan.*

Ask yourself:

- Are my assets up to date?
- Have my primary and contingent beneficiaries been clearly designated?
- Does my plan allow for restriction of a beneficiary?
- Does my legacy plan address minor children that I want to provide with income?
- Does my legacy plan allow for multi-generational payout?

Answers to these questions are critical if you want the final say in how your assets are distributed. In order to achieve your legacy goals, you need a plan.

MAKING A PLAN

Eventually, when your income need is filled and you have sufficient standby money to meet your need for emergencies, travel or other extra expenses you are planning for, whatever isn't used during your lifetime becomes your financial legacy. The money that you do not use during your lifetime will either go to loved ones, unloved ones, charity, or the IRS. The question is, who would you rather disinherit?

By having a legacy plan that clearly outlines your assets, your beneficiaries and your distribution goals, you can make sure that your money and property is ending up in the hands of the people you determine beforehand. Is it really that big of a deal? It absolutely is. Think about it. Without a clear plan, it is impossible for anyone to know if your beneficiary designations are current and reflect your wishes because you haven't clearly expressed who your beneficiaries are. You may have an idea of who you want your assets to go to, but without a plan, it is anyone's guess. It is also impossible to know if the titling of your assets is accurate unless you have gone through and determined whose name is on the titles. More importantly, *if you have not clearly and effectively communicated your desires regarding the planned distribution of your legacy, you and your family may end up losing a large part of it.*

As you can see, managing a legacy is more complicated than having an attorney read your will, divide your estate and write checks to your heirs. The additional issue of taxes, Family Maximum Benefit calculations and a host of other decisions rear their heads. Educating yourself about the best options for positioning your legacy assets is a challenging undertaking. Working with a financial professional who is versed in determining the most efficient and effective ways of preserving and distributing your legacy can save you time, money and strife.

So, how do you begin?

Making a Legacy Plan Starts with a Simple List. The first, and one of the largest, steps to setting up an estate plan with a financial professional that reflects your desires is creating a detailed inventory of your assets and debts (if you have any). You need to know what assets you have, who the beneficiaries are, how much they are worth and how they are titled. You can start by identifying and listing your assets. This is a good starting point for working with a financial professional who can then help you determine the detailed information about your assets that will dictate how they are distributed upon your death.

If you are particularly concerned about leaving your kids and grandkids a lifetime of income with minimal taxes, you will want to discuss a Stretch IRA option with your financial professional.

STRETCH IRAS: GETTING THE MOST OUT OF YOUR MONEY

In 1986, the U.S. Congress passed a law that allows for multi-generational distributions of IRA assets. This type of distribution is called a Stretch IRA because it stretches the distribution of the account out over a longer period of time to several beneficiaries. It also allows the account to continue accumulating value throughout your relatives' lifetimes. You can use a Stretch IRA as an income tool that distributes throughout your lifetime, your children's lifetimes and your grandchildren's lifetimes.

Stretch IRAs are an attractive option for those more concerned with creating income for their loved ones than leaving them with a lump sum that may be subject to a high tax rate. With traditional IRA distributions, non-spousal beneficiaries must generally take distributions from their inherited IRAs, whether transferred or not, within five years after the death of the IRA owner. An exception to this rule applies if the beneficiary elects to take distributions over his or her lifetime, which is referred to as stretching the IRA.

Beneficiaries Stretch IRA Distributions

Mr. Cleaver's IRA Value at 64: $350,000	Mr. Cleaver's income from age 70-85: $383,251	Mr. Cleaver passes away at 85
Mrs. Cleaver passes away at 88	Mrs. Cleaver's income from age 83-88: $180,048	Mrs. Cleaver's IRA Value: $453,165

| Wally receives income of: $133,971* | Beaver receives income of: $144,008* | Eddie receives income of: $293,717* | Lumpy receives income of: $313,799* | Gilbert receives income of: $345,752* |

TOTAL INCOME TO ALL - IRA STRETCH CONCEPT: $1,231,248
Scenario assumes a 28 percent tax rate with annual rate of return of 5 percent
*Income based on RMDs of beneficiaries

Beneficiaries FAIL to Stretch IRA Distributions

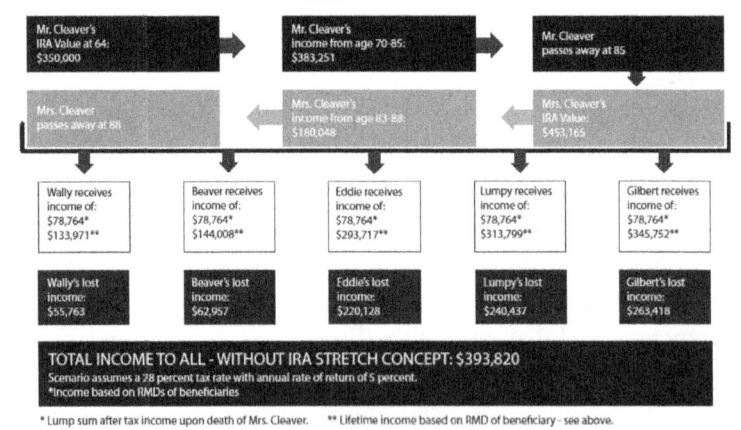

Mr. Cleaver's IRA Value at 64: $350,000	Mr. Cleaver's income from age 70-85: $383,251	Mr. Cleaver passes away at 85
Mrs. Cleaver passes away at 88	Mrs. Cleaver's income from age 83-88: $180,048	Mrs. Cleaver's IRA Value: $453,165

| Wally receives income of: $78,764* $133,971** | Beaver receives income of: $78,764* $144,008** | Eddie receives income of: $78,764* $293,717** | Lumpy receives income of: $78,764* $313,799** | Gilbert receives income of: $78,764* $345,752** |
| Wally's lost income: $55,763 | Beaver's lost income: $62,957 | Eddie's lost income: $220,128 | Lumpy's lost income: $240,437 | Gilbert's lost income: $263,418 |

TOTAL INCOME TO ALL - WITHOUT IRA STRETCH CONCEPT: $393,820
Scenario assumes a 28 percent tax rate with annual rate of return of 5 percent.
*Income based on RMDs of beneficiaries

* Lump sum after tax income upon death of Mrs. Cleaver. ** Lifetime income based on RMD of beneficiary - see above.

Let's begin by looking at the potential of stretching an IRA throughout multiple generations.

As the illustrations with the Cleaver family show, stretching an IRA over multiple generations can have a large impact on the total amount of income that it is able to provide. In the top illustration, Mr. Cleaver's IRA is stretched so it provides his children with multiple distributions throughout their lifetimes. By the time the account is empty, Mr. Cleaver's $350,000 IRA has been turned into a legacy of more than $1.2 million for the entire Cleaver family. But look at what happens when the IRA is not stretched: after Mr. and Mrs. Cleaver pass away, the IRA is divided between the five children and distributed to each as a single lump sum. In that scenario, the IRA only provides the Cleaver family with a total income of $393,820. For the Cleavers, not choosing to stretch the IRA would cost them nearly $800,000 in lost income.

Unfortunately, many things may also play a role in failing to stretch IRA distributions. It can be tempting for a beneficiary to take a lump sum of money despite the tax consequences. Fortunately, if you want to solidify your plan for distribution, there are options that will allow you to open up an IRA and incorporate "spendthrift" clauses for your beneficiaries. This will ensure your legacy is stretched appropriately and to your specifications. Only certain insurance companies allow this option, and you will not find this benefit with any brokerage accounts. You need to work with a financial professional who has the appropriate relationship with an insurance company that provides this option.

THE IRA TRUST: CONTROL YOUR ACCOUNTS FROM THE GRAVE

Establishing a Living Trust can be an effective way to avoid the expense and publicity of probate, but most living trusts are for non-IRA assets such as your house and property. In general, IRAs should not be placed in a Living Trust as they are typically not written with the very specific and complex language needed to comply with IRS rules. If improperly attempted, the beneficiaries of the IRA can be forced by the IRS to withdraw all the funds immediately making it all taxable. Designated beneficiaries are the common method to pass IRA assets. If setup and managed properly, the beneficiary can stretch the tax deferral properties of these funds over their lifetime. However, even having the correct designations and stretch options, this strategy can backfire if the beneficiary inadvertently or purposely choses to take the lump sum instead. Additionally, non-spousal beneficiaries who receive your IRA funds lose the same protections you, the IRA owner, has. Therefore, creditors (credit cards, student loans, etc.), lawsuits, and even divorce could cause your beneficiary to lose some or all of the IRA funds you passed to them.

One way to solve these issues and get both asset protection and guaranteed control of the stretch-out option is to set up something called The IRA Inheritance Trust®. This is a revocable trust separate from your Living Trust and designed specially for your IRAs, established by you, the owner. The IRA Trust offers two primary benefits:

Ensures that the IRA is stretched out to your specifications, which may or may not include beneficiary restrictions. So, to translate this into a real-life scenario: imagine your darling grandson all grown up. He moves to California, joins a rock band and develops what you suspect is a drug habit. You want him to remember you and to have this gift of money, but you don't want him to spend it all on hookers and cocaine. While this is said somewhat tongue-in-cheek, the point here is that you can make the choice to force the stretch of the IRA by establishing rules as to the distribution of this money. This gives you a way to effectively control the IRA from the grave, so to speak.

Offers asset protection from in-laws and creditors. Even if you have your IRA set up with proper designations for a stretch option, in cases of divorce, the IRA becomes vulnerable to issues. To translate this into a real-life scenario, imagine your daughter goes through an ugly divorce. Now the IRA money you have designated to go to her and her two daughters is no longer protected, because your daughter's ex-spouse legally has rights to this money.

When an IRA is set up inside this specially designed trust, it is no longer subject to issues with divorce, creditors or lawsuits.

The IRA Inheritance Trust® we use has been vetted by the IRS with an official Letter Ruling and has had hundreds of successful implementations. However, not all law firms own the rights to use this specially designed trust. Ask your investment advisor if your IRA is protected, and if he or she works with a law firm that can get you into one of these specially designed trusts.

CHAPTER 12 TAKE-AWAY //

- If you own an IRA, be aware that your beneficiaries could lose their inherited IRA to creditors, ex-spouses or cause them to pay higher taxes to Uncle Sam. Take action now and establish an IRA Inheritance Trust®.

13
PREPARING YOUR LEGACY

"Anyone who keeps learning stays young."
– Henry Ford

Jim organized his assets long ago. He started planning his retirement early and made investment decisions that would meet his needs. With a combination of IRA to Roth IRA conversions, a series of income annuities and a well-planned money management strategy overseen by his financial professional, he easily filled his income gap and was able to focus on ways to accumulate his wealth throughout his retirement. He reorganized his Know So and Hope So Money as he got older. When Jim retired, he had an income plan created that allowed him to maximize his Social Security benefit. He even had enough to accumulate wealth during his retirement. At this point, Jim turned his attention to planning his legacy. He wanted to know how he could maximize the amount of his legacy he will pass on to his heirs.

Jim met with an attorney to draw up a will, but he quickly learned that while having a will was a good plan, it wasn't the most efficient way to distribute his legacy. In fact, relying solely on a will created several roadblocks.

The two main problems that arose for Jim were *Probate* and *Unintentional Disinheritance:*

Problem #1: Probate
Probate. Just speaking the word out loud can cause shivers to run down your spine. Probate's ugly reputation is well deserved. It can be a costly, time consuming process that diminishes your estate and can delay the distribution of your estate to your loved ones. Nasty stuff, by any measure. Unless you have made a clear legacy plan and discussed options for avoiding probate, it is highly likely that you have many assets that might pass through probate needlessly. ***If your will and beneficiary designations aren't correctly structured, some of these assets will go through the probate process, which can turn dollars into cents.***

If you have a will, probate is usually just a formality. There is little risk that your will won't be executed per your instructions. The problem arises when the costs and lengthy timeline that probate creates come into play. Probate proceedings are notoriously expensive, lengthy and ponderous. A typical probate process identifies all of your assets and debts, pays any taxes and fees that you owe (including estate tax), pays court fees, and distributes your property and assets to your inheritors. This process usually takes at least a year, and can take even longer before your inheritors actually receive anything that you have left for them. For this reason, and because of the sometimes exorbitant fees that may be charged by lawyers and accountants during the process, probate has earned a nasty reputation.

Probate can also be a painstakingly public process. Because the probate process happens in court, the assets you own that go through a probate procedure become part of the public record. While this may not seem like a big deal to some, other people don't want that kind of intimate information available to the public.

Additionally, if your estate is entirely distributed via your will, the money that your family may need to cover the costs of your medical bills, funeral expenses and estate taxes will be tied up in probate, which can last up to a year or more. While immediate family members may have the option of requesting immediate cash from your assets during probate to cover immediate health care expenses, taxes, and fees, that process comes with its own set of complications. Choosing alternative methods for distributing your legacy can make life easier for your loved ones and can help them claim more of your estate in a more timely fashion than traditional methods.

A simpler and less tedious approach is to avoid probate altogether by structuring your estate to be distributed outside of the probate process. Two common ways of doing this are by structuring your assets inside a life insurance plan, and by using individual retirement planning tools like IRAs that give you the option of designating a beneficiary upon your death.

Problem #2: Unintentionally Disinheriting Your Family
You would never want to unintentionally disinherit a loved one or loved ones because of confusion surrounding your legacy plan. Unfortunately, it happens. Why? This terrible situation is typically caused by a simple lack of understanding. In particular, mistakes regarding legacy distribution occur with regards to those whom people care for the most: their grandchildren.

One of the most important ways to plan for the inheritance of your grandchildren is by properly structuring the distribution of your legacy. Specifically, you need to know if your legacy is going to be distributed *per stirpes* or *per capita*.

Per Stirpes. *Per stirpes* is a legal term in Latin that means "by the branch." Your estate will be distributed *per stirpes* if you designate each branch of your family to receive an equal share of your estate. In the event that your children predecease you, their share will be distributed evenly between their children—your grandchildren.

Per Capita. *Per capita* distribution is different in that you may designate different amounts of your estate to be distributed to members of the same generation.

Per stirpes distribution of assets will follow the family tree down the line as the predecessor beneficiaries pass away. On the other hand, per capita distribution of assets ends on the branch of the family tree with the death of a designated beneficiary. For example, when your child passes away, in a per capita distribution, your grandchildren would not receive distributions from the assets that you designated to your child.

What the terms mean is not nearly as important as what they do, however. The reality is that improperly titled assets could accidentally leave your grandchildren disinherited upon the death of their parents. It's easy to check, and it's even easier to fix.

A simple way to remember the difference between the two types of distribution goes something like this: "***Stirpes are forever and Capita is capped.***"

Another way to avoid complicated legacy distribution problems, and the probate process, is by leveraging a life insurance plan.

LIFE INSURANCE: AN IMPORTANT LEGACY TOOL

One of the most powerful legacy tools you can leverage is a good life insurance policy. Life insurance is a highly efficient legacy tool because it creates money when it is needed or desired the most. Over the years, life insurance has become less expensive, while it offers more features, and it provides longer guarantees.

There are many unique benefits of life insurance that can help your beneficiaries get the most out of your legacy. Some of them include:
- Providing beneficiaries with a tax-free, liquid asset.
- Covering the costs associated with your death.
- Providing income for your dependents.
- Offering an investment opportunity for your beneficiaries.
- Covering expenses such as tuition or mortgage down payments for your children or grandchildren.

Very few people want life insurance, but nearly everyone wants what it does. Life insurance is specifically, and uniquely, capable of creating money when it is needed most. When a loved one passes, no amount of money can remove the pain of loss. And certainly, money doesn't solve the challenges that might arise with losing someone important.

It has been said that when you have money, you have options. When you don't have money, your options are severely limited. You might imagine a life insurance policy can give your family and loved ones options that would otherwise be impossible.

> *» Maurice spent the last 20 years building a small business. In so many ways, it is a family business. Each of his three children, Maddie, Ruby and Caleb, worked in the shop part-time during high school. But after all three attended college, only Maddie returned to join her father, and eventually will run the business full-time when Maurice retires.*
>
> *Maurice is able to retire comfortably on Social Security and on-going income from the shop, but the business is nearly his entire financial legacy. It is his wish that Maddie own the*

business outright, but he also wants to leave an equal legacy to each of his three children.

There is no simple way to divide the business into thirds and still leave the business intact for Maddie.

Maurice ends up buying a life insurance policy to make up the difference. Ruby and Caleb will receive their share of an inheritance in cash from the life insurance policy and Maddie will be able to inherit the business intact.

Maurice is able to accomplish his goals, treat all three children equitably and leave Maddie the business she helped to build.

If you have a life insurance policy but you haven't looked at it in a while, you may not know how it operates, how much it is worth and how it will be distributed to your beneficiaries. You may also need to update your beneficiaries on your policy. In short, without a comprehensive review of your policy, you don't really know where the money will go or to whom it will go.

If you don't have a life insurance policy but are looking for options to maintain and grow your legacy, speaking with a professional can show you the benefits of life insurance. Many people don't consider buying a life insurance policy until some event in their life triggers it, like the loss of a loved one, an accident or a health condition.

BENEFITS OF LIFE INSURANCE

Life insurance is a useful and secure tool for contingency planning, ensuring that your dependents receive the assets that you want them to have, and for meeting the financial goals you have set for the future. While it bears the name "Life Insurance," it is, in reality, a diverse financial tool that can meet many needs. The main function of a life insurance policy is to provide financial assets for your survivors. Life insurance is particularly efficient at achieving this goal because it provides a tax-advantaged lump sum of money in the form of a death benefit to your beneficiary or beneficiaries. That financial asset can be used in a number of ways. It can be structured as an investment to provide income for your spouse or children, it can pay down debts, and it can be used to cover estate taxes and other costs associated with death.

Tax liabilities on the estate you leave behind are inevitable. Capital property, for instance, is taxed at its fair market value at the time of your death, unless that property is transferred to your spouse. If the property has appreciated during the time you owned it, taxation on capital gains will occur. Registered Retirement Savings Plans (RRSPs) and other similarly structured assets are also included as taxable income unless transferred to a beneficiary as well. Those are just a few examples of how an estate can become subject to a heavy tax burden. The unique benefits of a life insurance policy provide ways to handle this tax burden, solving any liquidity problems that may arise if your family members want to hold onto an illiquid asset, such as a piece of property or an investment. Life insurance can provide a significant amount of money to a family member or other beneficiary, and that money is likely to remain exempt from taxation or seizure.

One of life insurance's most important benefits is that it is not considered part of the estate of the policy holder. The death benefit that is paid by the insurance company goes exclusively to the beneficiaries listed on the policy. This shields the proceeds of the policy from fees and costs that can reduce an estate, including probate proceedings, attorneys' fees and claims made by creditors. The distribution of your life insurance policy is also unaffected by delays of the estate's distribution, like probate. Your beneficiaries will get the proceeds of the policy in a timely fashion, regardless of how long it takes for the rest of your estate to be settled.

Investing a portion of your assets in a life insurance policy can also protect that portion of your estate from creditors. If you owe money to someone or some entity at the time of your death, a creditor is not able to claim any money from a life insurance policy or an annuity, for that matter. An exception to this rule is if you had already used the life insurance policy as collateral against a loan. If a large portion of the money you want to dedicate to your legacy is sitting in a savings account, investment or other liquid form, creditors may be able to receive their claim on it before your beneficiaries get anything that is if there's anything left. A life insurance policy protects your assets from creditors and ensures that your beneficiaries get the money that you intend them to have.

HOW MUCH LIFE INSURANCE DO YOU NEED?

Determining the type of policy and the amount right for you depends on an analysis of your needs. A financial professional can help you complete a needs analysis that will highlight the amount of insurance that you require to meet your goals. This type of personalized review will allow you to determine ways to continue providing income for your spouse or any dependents you may have. A financial professional can also help you calculate the amount of income that your policy should replace to meet the needs of your beneficiaries and the duration of the distribution of that income.

You may also want to use your life insurance policy to meet any expenses associated with your death. These can include funeral costs, fees from probate and legal proceedings, and taxes. You may also want to dedicate a portion of your policy proceeds to help fund tuition or other expenses for your children or grandchildren. You can buy a policy and hope it covers all of those costs, or you can work with a professional who can calculate exactly how much insurance you need and how to structure it to meet your goals. Which would you rather do?

AVOIDING POTENTIAL SNAGS

There are benefits to having life insurance supersede the direction given in a will or other estate plan, but there are also some potential snags that you should address to meet your wishes. For example, if your will instructs that your assets be divided equally between your two children but your life insurance beneficiary is listed as just one of the children, the assets in the life insurance policy will only be distributed to the child listed as the beneficiary. The beneficiary designation of your life insurance supersedes your will's instruction. This is important to understand when designating beneficiaries on a policy you purchase. Work with a professional to make sure that your beneficiaries are accurately listed on your assets, especially your life insurance policies.

USING LIFE INSURANCE TO BUILD YOUR LEGACY

Depending on your goals, there are strategies you can use that could multiply how much you leave behind. Life insurance is one of the most surefire and efficient investment tools for building a substantial legacy that will meet your financial goals.

Here is a brief overview of how life insurance can boost your legacy:

- Life insurance provides an immediate increase in your legacy.
- It provides an income tax-advantaged death benefit for your beneficiaries.
- A good life insurance policy has the opportunity to accumulate value over time.
- It may have an option to include long-term care (LTC) or chronic illness benefits should you require them.

If your Green Money income needs for retirement are met and you have Yellow Money assets that will provide for your future expenses, you may have extra assets that you want to earmark as legacy funds. By electing to invest those assets into a life insurance policy, you can immediately increase the amount of your legacy. Remember, **life insurance allows you to transfer a tax-advantaged lump sum of money to your beneficiaries. It remains in your control during your lifetime, can provide for your long-term care needs and bypasses probate costs.** And make no mistake, taxes can have a huge impact on your legacy. Not only that, income and assets from your legacy can have tax implications for your beneficiaries, as well.

Here's a brief overview of how taxes could affect your legacy and your beneficiaries:
- The higher your income, the higher the rate at which it is taxed.
- Withdrawals from qualified plans are taxed as income.
- What's more, when you leave a large qualified plan, it ends up being taxed at a high rate.
- If you left a $500,000 IRA to your child, they could end up owing as much as $140,000 in income taxes.
- However, if you could just withdraw $50,000 a year, the tax bill might only be $10,000 per year.

How could you use that annual amount to leave a larger legacy? Luckily, you can leverage a life insurance policy to avoid those tax penalties, preserving a larger amount of your legacy and freeing your beneficiaries from an added tax burden.

> *» When Beverly turned 70 years old, she decided it was time to look into life insurance policy options. She still feels young, but she remembers that her mother died in early 70s, and she wants to plan ahead so she can pass on some of her legacy to her grandchildren just like her grandmother did for her.*
>
> *Beverly doesn't really want to think about life insurance, but she does want the security, reliability and tax-advantaged*

distribution that it offers. She lives modestly, and her Social Security benefit meets most of her income needs. As the beneficiary of her late husband's Certificate of Deposit (CD), she has $100,000 in an account that she has never used and doesn't anticipate ever needing since her income needs were already met.

*After looking at several different investment options with a professional, Beverly decides that a Single Premium life insurance policy fits her needs best. She can buy the policy with a $100,000 one-time payment and she is guaranteed that it would provide more than the value of the contract to her beneficiaries. If she left the money in the CD, it would be subject to taxes. But for every dollar that she puts into the life insurance policy, her beneficiaries are guaranteed at least that dollar plus a death benefit, and all of it will be **tax-free!***

For $100,000, Beverly's particular policy offers a $170,000 death benefit distribution to her beneficiaries. By moving the $100,000 from a CD to a life insurance policy, Beverly increases her legacy by 70 percent. Not only that, she has also sheltered it from taxes, so her beneficiaries will be able to receive $1.70 for every $1.00 that she entered into the policy! While buying the policy doesn't allow her to use the money for herself, it does allow her family to benefit from her well-planned legacy.

MAKE YOUR WISHES KNOWN

Estate taxes used to be a much hotter topic in the mid-2000s when the estate tax limits and exclusions were much smaller and taxed at a higher rate than today. In 2008, estates valued at $2 million or more were taxed at 45 percent. Just two years later, the limit was raised to $5 million dollars taxed at 35 percent. The limit has continued to rise ever since. The limit applies to fewer people than before. Estate organization, however, is just as important as ever, and it affects everyone.

Ask yourself:
- Are your assets actually titled and held the way you think they are?
- Are your beneficiaries set up the way you think they should be?
- Have there been changes to your family or those you desire as beneficiaries?

There is more to your legacy beyond your property, money, investments and other assets that you leave to family members, loved ones and charities. Everyone has a legacy beyond money. You also leave behind personal items of importance, your values and beliefs, your personal and family history, and your wishes. Beyond a will and a plan for your assets, it is important that you make your wishes known to someone for the rest of your personal legacy. When it comes time for your family and loved ones to make decisions after you are gone, knowing your wishes can help them make decisions that honor you and your legacy, and give meaning to what you leave behind. Your professional can help you organize.

Think about your:
- Personal stories / recollections
- Values
- Personal items of emotional significance
- Financial assets

Do you want to make a plan to pass these things on to your family?

WORKING WITH A PROFESSIONAL

Part of using life insurance to your greatest advantage is selecting the policy and provider that can best meet your goals. Venturing into the jungle of policies, brokers and salespeople can be overwhelming, and can leave you wondering if you've made the best decision. Working with a trusted financial professional can help you cut through the red tape, the "sales-speak" and confusion to find a policy that meets your goals and best serves your desires for your money. If you already have a policy, a financial professional can help you review it and become familiar with the policy's premium, the guarantees the policy affords, its performance, and its features and benefits. A financial professional can also help you make any necessary changes to the policy.

> » *When Sue turned 88, her daughter finally convinced her to meet with a financial professional to help her organize her assets and get her legacy in order. Although Sue is reluctant to let a stranger in on her personal finances, she ends up very glad that she did.*
>
> *In the process of listing Sue's assets and her beneficiaries, her professional finds a man's name listed as the beneficiary of an old life insurance annuity that she owns. It turns out, the man is Sue's ex-husband who is still alive. Had Sue passed away before her ex-husband, the annuities and any death benefits that came with them, would have been passed on to her ex-husband. This does not reflect her latest wishes.*

Things change, relationships evolve and the way you would like your legacy organized needs to adapt to the changes that happen throughout your life. There may be a new child or grandchild in your family, or you may have been divorced or remarried. A professional will regularly review your legacy assets and ask you questions to make sure that everything is up to date and that the current organization reflects your current wishes.

CHAPTER 13 TAKE-AWAY //
- Anybody who loves somebody should consider the benefits that life insurance can offer, both as a way to build your legacy and as reimbursement for long-term care expenses offered by flexible premium life insurance policies.

14

FINDING A FINANCIAL PROFESSIONAL WHO HAS INTEGRITY

"Character is like 'Structural Integrity' in the field of engineering. A construction is believed to have structural integrity when it can withstand 'impact' from anywhere and anything, functioning adequately for its desired purposes and service in life, until a physical collapse proves otherwise."
– Olaotan Fawehinmi, The Soldier Within

From the moment you dip your toes into the retirement planning pool to the point you start swimming laps, your assets organized, your income needs met, and your accumulation and legacy plans in place, working with a professional that you trust can make all the difference in how well your retirement reflects your desires.

It is important to know what you are looking for before taking the plunge. There are many people that would love to handle your money, but not everyone is qualified to handle it in a way that leads to a holistic approach to creating a solid retirement plan.

The distinction being made here is that you should look for someone that puts your interests first and actively wants to help you meet your goals and objectives. Oftentimes, the products someone sells you matter less than their dedication to making sure that you have a plan that meets your needs.

Professionals who have integrity take your whole financial position into consideration. They make plans that adjust your risk exposure, invest in tools that secure your desired income during retirement and create investment strategies that allow you to continue accumulating wealth during your retirement for you to use later or to contribute to your legacy. If you buy stocks with a broker, use a different agent for a life insurance policy and have an unmanaged 401(k) through your employer, working with a financial professional will consolidate the management of your assets so you have one trustworthy person quarterbacking all of the team elements of your portfolio. Financial products and investment tools change, but the concepts that lie behind wise retirement planning are lasting. In the end, a financial professional's approach is designed for those serious about planning for retirement. *Can you say the same thing about the person that advises you about your financial life?*

It's easy to see how choosing a financial professional can be one of the most important decisions you can make in your life. Not only do they provide you with advice, they also manage the personal assets that supply your retirement income and contribute to your legacy. So, how do you find a good one?

HOW TO FIND A FINANCIAL PROFESSIONAL YOU CAN TRUST

Taking care to select a financial professional is one of the best things you can do for yourself and for your future. Your professional has influence and control of your investment decisions, making their role in your life more than just important. Your financial security and the quality of your retirement depends on the decisions, investment strategies and asset structuring that you and your professional create.

Working with a professional is different than calling up a broker when you want to buy or trade some stock. This isn't a decision that you can hand off to anyone else. You need to bring your time and attention to the table when it comes to finding someone with whom you can entrust your financial life. Separating the wheat from the chaff will take some work, but you'll be happy you did it.

While no one can tell you exactly who to choose or how to choose them, the following information can help you narrow the field:

- You can start by asking your friends, family and colleagues for referrals. You will want to pay particular attention to the recommendations that you get from others who are in your similar financial situation and who have similar lifestyle choices. The professional for the CEO of your company may have a different skill-set than the skill-set of the professional befitting your cousin who has 3 kids and a Subaru like you. Do follow-up research on the Internet as well. Look up the people who have been recommended to you on websites like LinkedIn that show the work history, referrals and experience of the candidates that you find most attractive. You will also learn about the firms with or for whom they work. The investment philosophies and reputations of the companies they work for will tell you a lot about how they will handle your money.

- The other side of the coin, however, is that everyone and their brother has a recommendation about how you should manage your money and who should manage it for you. From hot stock tips to "the best money manager in the state," people love to share good information that makes them look like they are in-the-know. Nobody wants to talk about the bad stock purchases they made, the times they lost money and the poor selections they made regarding financial professionals or stock brokers. If you decide to take a friend or family member's recommendation, make sure they have a substantial, long-term experience with the financial professional and that their glowing review isn't just based on a one-time "win."
- It is important to understand how your professional is being paid. It is generally considered preferable to work with a fee-based professional who will not have conflicts of interests between earning a commission and acting in your best interests.
- Many professionals may also be brokers or dealers that can earn commissions on things like life insurance, certain types of annuities and disability insurance. These professionals have most likely intentionally overlapped their roles so that if their clients choose to purchase insurance or investment products that require a broker or dealer, those clients won't have to find an additional person to work with. Again, understanding the role of your professional will help you make your determination.

NARROWING THE FIELD
1. Decide on the Type of Professional with Whom You Want to Work. There are four basic kinds of financial professionals. Many professionals may play overlapping roles. It is important to

know a professional's primary function, how they charge for their services and whether they are obligated to act in your best interest. *Registered representatives*, better known as stockbrokers or bank / investment representatives, make their living by earning commissions on insurance products and investment services. Stockbrokers basically sell you things. The products from which they make the highest commission are sometimes the products that they recommend to their clients. If you want to make a simple transaction, such as buying or selling a particular stock, a registered representative can help you. Although registered representatives are licensed professionals, if you want to create a structured and planful approach to positioning your assets for retirement, you might want to consider continuing your search.

The term "planner" is often misused. It can refer to credible professionals that are CPAs, CFPs and ChFCs to your uncle's next door neighbor who claims to have a lead on some undervalued stock about to be "discovered." A wide array of people may claim to be planners because there are no requirements to be a planner. The term financial planner, however, refers to someone who is properly registered as an investment advisor and serves as a fiduciary as described below.

Financial professionals are the diamonds in the rough. These Registered Investment Advisors are compensated on a fee basis. They do, however, often have licensure as stockbrokers or insurance agents, allowing them to earn commissions on certain transactions. More importantly, **financial professionals are financial fiduciaries, meaning they are required to make financial decisions in your best interest and reflecting your risk tolerance.** Investment Advisors are held to high ethical standards and are highly regarded in the financial industry. Financial professionals also often take a more comprehensive approach to asset management. These professionals are trained and credentialed to plan and coordinate their clients' assets in order to meet their goals or retirement and legacy planning. They are not focused on individual stocks, investments or markets. They look at the big picture, the whole enchilada.

Money managers are on par with financial professionals. However, they are often given explicit permission to make investment decisions without advanced approval by their clients.

Understanding who you are working with and what their title is the first step to planning your retirement. While each of the above-mentioned types of financial professionals can help you with aspects of your finances, it is **financial professionals** who have the most intimate role, the most objective investment strategies and the most unbiased mode of compensation for their services. A financial professional can also help you with the non-financial aspects of your legacy and can help you find ways to create a tax planning strategy to help you save money.

2. Be Objective. At the end of the day, you need to separate the weak from the strong. While you might want a strong personal rapport with your professional, or you may want to choose your professional for their personality and positive attitude, it is more important that you find someone who will give sage advice regarding achieving your retirement goals.

It can be helpful to use a process of elimination to narrow the field of potential professionals. Look into five or six potential leads and cross off your list the ones that don't meet your requirements until only one or two remain. Cross-check your remaining choices against the list of things you need from a professional. Make sure they represent a firm that has the investment tools and products that you desire, and make sure they have experience in retirement planning. That is, after all, the main goal.

Don't be afraid to investigate each of your candidates. You'll want to ask the same questions and look for the same information from everyone you consider so you can then compare them and discern which is best for you. You'll want to take a look at the specific credentials of each professional, their experience and competence, their ethics and fiduciary status, their history and track record, and a list of the services that they offer. The professionals who meet all or most of your qualifications are the ones you will contact for an interview.

Potential professionals should meet your qualifications in the following categories:

- *Integrity:* Does your professional take the time to get to know you and listen to your concerns, or do they spend the meeting try to sell you on them, their company and the products or investments they offer? You can't rely on credentials and big names alone as indicators of integrity and good character.
- *Practices:* Look at the track record of your candidates, how they are compensated for their services, the reports and analysis they offer, and their value added services. Someone who has continued their professional education will be more up-to-date on current financial practices compared to someone who got their degree 25 years ago and hasn't done a thing since.
- *Services:* Your professional must meet your needs. If you are planning your retirement, you should work with someone who offers services that help you to that end. You want someone who can offer planning, advice on investment strategies, ways to calculate risk, advice on insurance and annuities products, and ways to manage your tax strategy.
- *Ethics:* You want to work with someone who is above board and does things the right way. Vet them by checking their compliance record, current licensing, fiduciary status and, yes, even their criminal record. You never know!

3. Use the Internet. As a final step before picking up the phone and calling your candidates, do some digging to discover if anyone on your list has a history of unlawful or unethical practices, or has been disciplined for any of their professional behavior or decisions. Don't worry, you don't have to hire a private investigator. You can easily find this information on the Financial Industry Regulatory Authority's (FINRA) online BrokerCheck tool: http://www.finra.org/Investors/ToolsCalculators/BrokerCheck/.

You should obviously explore the website of a potential professional and the website of the firm that they represent. The Internet allows you to go beyond the online business card of a professional to gain access to information that they don't control. It may all be good information! Or a brief search of the Internet could reveal a sketchy past. The best part is that the Internet allows you to find helpful information in an anonymous fashion.

Start with Google (www.google.com) and search the name of a potential professional and their firm. Keep your eyes trained on third party sources such as articles, blog posts or news stories that mention the professional. You can also check a professional's compliance records online with the Financial Industry Regulatory Authority (FINRA) and the Securities and Exchange Commission (SEC). If you want to dig deeper, you can combine search terms like "scams," "lawsuits," "suspensions" and "fraud" with a professional's or firm's name to see what information arises. More likely than not, you won't find anything. But if you do, you'll be glad that you checked.

HOW TO INTERVIEW CANDIDATES

After vetting your candidates and narrowing down a list of professionals that you think might be a good fit for you, it's time to start interviewing.

When you meet in person with a professional, you want to take advantage of your time with them. The presentations and information that they share with you will be important to pay attention to, but you will also want to control some aspects of the interview. After a professional has told you what they want you to hear, it's time to ask your own questions to get the specific information you need to make your decision.

Make sure to prepare a list of questions and an informal agenda so that you can keep track of what you want to ask and what points you want the professional to touch on during the interview. Using the same questions and agenda will also allow you to more easily compare the professionals after you have interviewed them all. Remember that these interviews are just that, *interviews*. You are meeting with several professionals to determine with whom you want to work. Don't agree to anything or sign anything during an interview until after you have made your final decision.

It can also be helpful to put a time limit on your interviews and to meet the professionals at their offices. The time limit will keep things on track and will allow structured time for presentations and questions/discussion. By meeting them at their office, you can get a sense of the work environment, the staff culture and attitude, and how the firm does business. If you are unable to travel to a professional's office and must meet them at your home or office, make sure that your interviews are scheduled with plenty of time between so the professionals don't cross each other's paths.

You can use the following questions during an initial interview to get an understanding of how each professional does business and whether they are a good fit for you:

1. How do you charge for your services? How much do you charge? This information should be easy to find on their website, but if you don't see it, ask. Find out if they charge an initial planning fee, if they charge a percentage for assets under their management and if they make money by selling specific financial products or services. If so, you should follow up by asking how much the service costs. This will give you an idea of how they really make their money and if they have incentive to sell certain products over others. Make sure you understand exactly how you will be charged so there are no surprises down the road if you decide to work with this person.

2. Is your professional independent and held to the fiduciary standard? If you want someone to manage your money, you will most likely look for an Investment Advisor Representative, or IAR. Many financial professionals call themselves advisors, but only those with an IAR designation are legally obligated to help you make decisions that are in your best interest only. When a professional chooses to become an IAR, he or she does so knowing they will be held to the highest standards in the financial industry. An IAR that works with an independent firm will likely have a team of CPAs, CFPs and other financial experts upon whom they can draw. If you like the professional you are meeting with and you think they might be a good fit, but they don't have the experience you want them to have, ask about their firm and the resources available to them. If they work closely with experienced CPAs, legal attorneys and third-party money managers, it could be an excellent match a way to get a holistic plan where decisions among several professionals are coordinated to give you greater efficiency.

3. What are the financial services that you and your firm provide? To piggy-back on the above point, the question within the question here is, "Can you help me achieve my goals?" Some people can only provide you with investment advice, and others are tax consultants. You will likely want to work with someone that provides a complete suite of financial planning services and products that touch on retirement planning, insurance options, legacy and estate structuring, and tax planning. Whatever services they provide, make sure they meet your needs and your anticipated needs.

4. What kinds of clients do you work with the most? A lot of financial professionals work within a niche: retirement planning, risk assessment, life insurance, etc. Finding someone who works with other people that are in the same financial boat as you and who have similar goals can be an important way to make sure they understand your needs. While someone might be a crackerjack annuities cowboy, you might not be interested in that option. Ask follow-up questions that will really help you understand where their expertise lies and whether or not their experience lines up with your needs.

5. May I see a sample of one of your financial plans? You wouldn't buy a car without test driving it, and you should not work with a professional without seeing a sample of how they do business. While there is no formal structure that a financial plan has to follow, the variation between professionals can help you find someone who "speaks your language." One professional may provide you with an in-depth analysis that relies heavily on info graphics and diagrams. Someone else may give you a seven page review of your assets and general recommendations. By seeing a sample plan, you can narrow down who presents information in the way that you desire and in ways that you understand.

6. How do you approach investing? You may be entirely in the dark about how to approach your investments, or you might have some guiding principles. Either way, ask each candidate what their philosophy is. Some will resonate with you and some won't. A good professional who has a realistic approach to investing won't promise you the moon or tell you that they can make you a lot of money. Professionals who are successful at retirement planning and full service financial management will tell you that they will listen to your goals, risk tolerance and comfort level with different types of investment strategies. Working with someone that you trust is critical, and this question in particular can help you find out who you can and who you can't.

7. How do you remain in contact with your clients? Does your prospective professional hold annual, quarterly or monthly meetings? How often do *you* want to meet with your professional? Some people want to check in once a year, go over everything and make sure their ducks are all in a row. If any changes over the previous year or additions to their legacy planning strategy came up, they'll do it on that date. Other people want a monthly update to be more involved in the decision making process and to understand what's happening with their portfolio. You basically need to determine the right degree of involvement for both you and your financial professional. You'll also want to feel out how your professional communicates. Do you prefer phone calls or face-to-face meetings? Do you want your professional to explain things to you in detail or to summarize for you what decisions they've made? Is the professional willing to give you their direct phone number or their email address? More importantly, do you want that information and do you want to be able to contact them in those ways?

8. Are you my main contact, or do you work with a team? This is another way of finding out how involved with you your professional will be, and how often they will meet with you. It is also a way to discover how the firm they represent operates and manages their clients. Some professionals will answer their own phone, meet with you regularly and have your home phone number on speed dial. Others will meet with you once a year and have a partner or assistant check in with you every quarter to give you an update. Other companies take an entirely team-based approach whereby clients have a main contact but their portfolio is handled by a team of professionals that represent the firm. One way isn't better than another, but one way will be best for you. Find out how the professional you are interviewing operates before entering into an agreement.

9. How do you provide a unique experience for your clients? This is a polite way of asking, "Why should I work with you?" A professional should have a compelling answer to this question that connects with you. Their answer will likely touch on their investment philosophy, their communication style and their expertise. If you hear them describing strengths and philosophies that resonate with you, keep them on your list. Some professionals will tell you that they will make investments with your money that match your values, others will say they will maximize your returns and others will say they will protect your capital while structuring your assets for income. Whatever you're looking for in a professional, you will most likely find it in the answer to this question.

This last question you will want to ask *yourself* after you've met with someone who you are considering hiring:

10. Did they ask questions and show signs that they were interested in working with me? A professional who will structure your assets to reflect your risk tolerance and to position you for a comfortable retirement must be a good listener. You will want to pass by a professional who talks non-stop and tells you what to do without listening to what you want them to do. If you felt they listened well and understood your needs, and seemed interested and experienced in your situation, then they might be right for you.

THE IMPORTANCE OF INDEPENDENCE
Not all investment firms and financial professionals are created equal. The information in this book has systematically shown that leveraging investments for income and accumulation in today's market requires new ideas and modern planning. In short, you need innovative ideas to come up with the creative solutions that will provide you with the retirement that you want. Innovation thrives on independence. No matter how good a financial professional is, the firm that they represent needs to operate on principles that make sense in today's economy. Remember, advice about money has been around forever. Good advice, however, changes with the times.

Timing the market, relying on the sale of stocks for income and banking on high treasury and bond returns are not strategies. They aren't even realistic ways to make money or to generate income. Working with an independent agent can help you break free from the old ways of thinking and position you to create a realistic retirement plan.

Working with an independent professional who relies on fee-based income tied to the success of their performance will also give you greater peace of mind. When you do well, they do well, and that's the way it should be. Your independent financial professional will make sure that:

- Your assets are organized and structured to reflect your risk tolerance.
- Your assets will be available to you when you need them and in the way that you need them.
- You will have a lifetime income that will support your lifestyle through your retirement.
- You are handling your taxes as efficiently as possible.
- Your legacy is in order.
- Your Red Money is turned into Yellow Money, and is managed in your best interest.

» *Remember Mark and Kristi from Chapter 1? Even though they knew they had Social Security benefits coming, they placed some money in savings and each had a pension or a 401(k).* **Before they met with a financial professional, they had no idea what their retirement would look like.** *After they met with an agent, they knew exactly what types of assets they had, how much they were worth, how much risk they were exposed to and how they were going to be distributed. They also created an income plan so that they could pay their bills every month the moment they retired, and they maximized their Social Security benefit by targeting the year and month they would get the most lifetime benefits. After their income needs were met, they were able to continue accumulating wealth by investing their extra assets to serve them in the future and contribute to their legacy. Their professional also helped them make decisions that impacted their taxes, protecting the value of their assets and allowing them to keep more of their money.*

This isn't a fairy tale scenario. This is an example of how much you stand to gain by meeting with a financial professional who can help you create a planful approach to your retirement. The concept of Know So and Hope So didn't just apply to their money, it also applied to Mark and Kristi. They **hoped** that they would have enough for retirement and that they had worked hard enough and saved enough to maintain their lifestyle. Working with a financial professional allowed them to **know** that their income needs were secured and structured to provide them with income for the rest of their lives and with some money to spare.

Now, ask yourself: Is your retirement built on hopes and dreams, or a solid, predictable plan?

IT'S WORTH IT!

Finding, interviewing and selecting a financial professional can seem like a daunting task. And honestly, it will take a good amount of work to narrow the field and find the one you want. In the end, it is worth the blood, sweat and tears. Your retirement, lifestyle, assets and legacy is on the line. The choices you make today will have lasting impacts on your life and the life of your loved ones. Working with someone you trust and know to have integrity is invaluable. The work it takes to find them is something you will never regret.

CHAPTER 14 TAKE-AWAY //

- You only get to retire once. Taking the time to find an independent financial professional who has integrity means working with someone who will help guide you to make decisions that are always in your best interest.

GLOSSARY*

ANNUAL RESET *(ANNUAL RATCHET, CLIQUET)* – Crediting methods measuring index movement over a one year period. Positive interest is calculated and credited at the end of each contract year and cannot be lost if the index subsequently declines. Say that the index increased from 100 to 110 in one year and the indexed annuity had an 80 percent participation rate. The insurance company would take the 10 percent gross index gain for the year (110-100/100), apply the participation rate (10 percent index gain x 80 percent rate) and credit 8 percent interest to the annuity. But, what if in the following year the index declined back to 100? The individual would keep the 8 percent interest earned and simply receive zero interest for the down year. An annual reset structure

---

* *"Glossary of Terms." FixedAnnuityFacts.com. NAFA, the National Association for Fixed Annuities, n.d. 12 Nov. 2013*

preserves credited gains and treats negative index periods as years with zero growth.

ANNUITANT – The person, usually the annuity owner, whose life expectancy is used to calculate the income payment amount on the annuity.

ANNUITY – An annuity is a contract issued by an insurance company that often serves as a type of savings plan used by individuals looking for long term growth and protection of assets that will likely be needed within retirement.

AVERAGING – Index values may either be measured from a start point to an end point (point-to-point) or values between the start point and end point may be averaged to determine an ending value. Index values may be averaged over the days, weeks, months or quarters of the period.

BENEFICIARY – A beneficiary is the person designated to receive payments due upon the death of the annuity owner or the annuitant themselves.

BONUS RATE – A bonus rate is the "extra" or "additional" interest paid during the first year (the initial guarantee period), typically used as an added incentive to get consumers to select their annuity policy over another.

CALL OPTION *(ALSO SEE PUT OPTION)* – Gives the holder the right to buy an underlying security or index at a specified price on or before a given date.

CAP – The maximum interest rate that will be credited to the annuity for the year or period. The cap usually refers to the maximum interest credited after applying the participation rate or yield spread. If the index methodology showed a 20 percent increase, the participation rate was 60 percent and the maximum interest cap was 10 percent, the contract would credit 10 percent interest. A few annuities use a maximum gain cap instead of a maximum interest cap with the participation rate or yield spread applied to the lesser of the gain or the cap. If the index methodology showed a 20 percent increase, the participation rate was 60 percent and the maximum gain cap was 10 percent, the contract would credit 6 percent interest.

COMPOUND INTEREST – Interest is earned on both the original principal and on previously earned interest. It is more favorable than simple interest. Suppose that your original principal was $1 and your interest rate was 10 percent for five years. With simple interest, your value is ($1 + $0.10 interest each year) = $1.50. With compound interest, your value is ($1 x 1.10 x 1.10 x 1.10 x 1.10 x 1.10) = $1.61. The advantage of compound interest over simple interest becomes greater as each subsequent period passes.

CREDITING METHOD *(ALSO SEE METHODOLOGY)* – The formula(s) used to determine the excess interest that is credited above the minimum interest guarantee.

DEATH BENEFITS – The payment the annuity owner's estate or beneficiaries will receive if he or she dies before the annuity matures. On most annuities, this is equal to the current account value. Some annuities offer an enhanced value at death via an optional rider that has a monthly or annual fee associated with it.

EXCESS INTEREST – Interest credited to the annuity contract above the minimum guaranteed interest rate. In an indexed annuity the excess interest is determined by applying a stated crediting method to a specific index or indices.

FIXED ANNUITY – A contract issued by an insurance company guaranteeing a minimum interest rate with the crediting of excess interest determined by the performance of the insurer's general account. Index annuities are fixed annuities.

FIXED DEFERRED ANNUITY – With fixed annuities, an insurance company offers a guaranteed interest rate plus safety of your principal and earnings ((subject to the claims-paying ability of the insurance company). Your interest rate will be reset periodically, based on economic and other factors, but is guaranteed to never fall below a certain rate.

FREE WITHDRAWALS – Withdrawals that are free of surrender charges.

INDEX – The underlying external benchmark upon which the crediting of excess interest is based, also a measure of the prices of a group of securities.

IRA *(INDIVIDUAL RETIREMENT ACCOUNT)* – An IRA is a tax-advantaged personal savings plan that lets an individual set aside money for retirement. All or part of the participant's contributions may be tax deductible, depending on the type of IRA chosen and the participant's personal financial circumstances. Distributions from many employer-sponsored retirement plans may be eligible to be rolled into an IRA to continue tax-deferred growth until the funds are needed. An annuity can be used as an IRA; that is, IRA funds can be used to purchase an annuity.

IRA ROLLOVER – IRA rollover is the phrase used when an individual who has a balance in an employer-sponsored retirement plan transfers that balance into an IRA. Such an exchange, when properly handled, is a tax-advantaged transaction.

LIQUIDITY – The ease with which an asset is convertible to cash. An asset with high liquidity provides flexibility, in that the owner can easily convert it to cash at any time, but it also tends to decrease profitability.

MARKET RISK – The risk of the market value of an asset fluctuating up or down over time. In a fixed or fixed indexed annuity, the original principal and credited interest are not subject to market risk. Even if the index declines, the annuity owner would receive no less than their original principal back if they decided to cash in the policy at the end of the surrender period. Unlike a security, indexed annuities guarantee the original premium and the premium is backed by, and is as safe as, the insurance company that issued it (subject to the claims-paying ability of the insurance company).

METHODOLOGY *(ALSO SEE CREDITING METHOD)* – The way that interest crediting is calculated. On fixed indexed annuities, there are a variety of different methods used to determine how index movement becomes interest credited.

MINIMUM GUARANTEED RETURN *(MINIMUM INTEREST RATE)* – Fixed indexed annuities typically provide a minimum guaranteed return over the life of the contract. At the time that the owner chooses to terminate the contract, the cash surrender value is compared to a second value calculated using the minimum guaranteed return and the higher of the two values is paid to the annuity owner.

OPTION – A contract which conveys to its holder the right, but not the obligation, to buy or sell something at a specified price on or before a given date. After this given date the option ceases to exist. Insurers typically buy options to provide for the excess interest potential. Options may be American style whereby they may be exercised at any time prior to the given date, or they may have to be exercised only during a specified window. Options that may only be exercised during a specified period are European-style options.

OPTION RISK – Most insurers create the potential for excess interest in an indexed annuity by buying options. Say that you could buy a share of stock for $50. If you bought the stock and it rose to $60 you could sell it and net a $10 profit. But, if the stock price fell to $40 you'd have a $10 loss. Instead of buying the actual stock, we could buy an option that gave us the right to buy the stock for $50 at any time over the next year. The cost of the option is $2. If the stock price rose to $60 we would exercise our option, buy the stock at $50 and make $10 (less the $2 cost of the option). If the price of the stock fell to $40, $30 or $10, we wouldn't use the option and it would expire. The loss is limited to $2—the cost of the option.

PARTICIPATION RATE – The percentage of positive index movement credited to the annuity. If the index methodology determined that the index increased 10 percent and the indexed annuity participated in 60 percent of the increase, it would be said that the contract has a 60 percent participation rate. Participation rates may also be expressed as asset fees or yield spreads.

POINT-TO-POINT – A crediting method measuring index movement from an absolute initial point to the absolute end point for a period. An index had a period starting value of 100 and a period ending value of 120. A point-to-point method would record a positive index movement of 20 [120-100] or a 20 percent positive movement [(120-100)/100]. Point-to-point usually refers to annual periods; however the phrase is also used instead of term end point to refer to multiple year periods.

PREMIUM BONUS – A premium bonus is additional money that is credited to the accumulation account of an annuity policy under certain conditions.

PUT OPTION *(ALSO SEE CALL OPTION)* – Gives the holder the right to sell an underlying security or index at a specified price on or before a given date.

QUALIFIED ANNUITIES *(QUALIFIED MONEY)* – Qualified annuities are annuities purchased for funding an IRA, 403(b) tax-deferred annuity or other type of retirement arrangements. An IRA or qualified retirement plan provides the tax deferral. An annuity contract should be used to fund an IRA or qualified retirement plan to benefit from an annuity's features other than tax deferral, including the safety features, lifetime income payout option and death benefit protection.

REQUIRED MINIMUM DISTRIBUTION *(RMD)* – The amount of money that Traditional, SEP and SIMPLE IRA owners and qualified plan participants must begin distributing from their retirement accounts by April 1 following the year they reach age 70.5. RMD amounts must then be distributed each subsequent year.

RETURN FLOOR – Another way of saying minimum guaranteed return.

ROTH IRA – Like other IRA accounts, the Roth IRA is simply a holding account that manages your stocks, bonds, annuities, mutual funds and CD's. However, future withdrawals (including earnings and interest) are typically tax-advantaged once the account has been open for five years and the account holder is age 59.5.

RULE OF 72 – Tells you approximately how many years it takes a sum to double at a given rate. It's handy to be able to figure out, without using a calculator, that when you're earning a 6 percent return, for example, by dividing 6 percent into 72, you'll find that it takes 12 years for money to double. Conversely, if you know it took a sum twelve years to double you could divide 12 into 72 to determine the annual return (6 percent).

SIMPLE INTEREST *(ALSO SEE COMPOUND INTEREST)* – Interest is only earned on the principal balance.

SPLIT ANNUITY – A split annuity is the term given to an effective strategy that utilizes two or more different annuity products—one designed to generate monthly income and the other to restore the original starting principal over a set period of time.

STANDARD & POOR'S 500 *(S&P 500)* – The most widely used external index by fixed indexed annuities. Its objective is to be a benchmark to measure and report overall U.S. stock market performance. It includes a representative sample of 500 common stocks from companies trading on the New York Stock Exchange, American Stock Exchange, and NASDAQ National Market System. The index represents the price or market value of the underlying stocks and does not include the value of reinvested dividends of the underlying stocks.

STOCK MARKET INDEX – A report created from a type of statistical measurement that shows up or down changes in a specific financial market, usually expressed as points and as a percentage, in a number of related markets, or in an economy as a whole (i.e. S&P 500 or New York Stock Exchange).

SURRENDER CHARGE – A charge imposed for withdrawing funds or terminating an annuity contract prematurely. There is no industry standard for surrender charges, that is, each annuity product has its own unique surrender charge schedule. The charge is usually expressed as a percentage of the amount withdrawn prematurely from the contract. The percentage tends to decline over time, ultimately becoming zero.

TRADITIONAL IRA – SEE IRA (INDIVIDUAL RETIREMENT ACCOUNT)

TERM END POINT – Crediting methods measuring index movements over a greater timeframe than a year or two. The opposite of an annual reset method. Also referred to as a term point-to-point method. Say that the index value was at 100 on the first day of the period. If the calculated index value was at 150 at the end of the period the positive index movement would be 50 percent (150-100/100). The company would credit a percentage of this movement as excess interest. Index movement is calculated and interest credited at the end of the term and interim movements during the period are ignored.

TERM HIGH POINT *(HIGH WATER MARK)* – A type of term end point structure that uses the highest anniversary index level as the end point. Say that the index value was at 100 on the first day of the period, reached a value of 160 at the end of a contract year during the period, and ended the period at 150. A term high point method would use the 160 value—the highest contract anniversary point reached during the period, as the end point and the gross index gain would be 60 percent (160-100/100). The company would then apply a participation rate to the gain.

TERM YIELD SPREAD – A type of term end point structure which calculates the total index gain for a period, computes the annual compound rate of return deducts a yield spread from the annual rate of return and then recalculates the total index gain for the period based on the net annual rate. Say that an index increased from 100 to 200 by the end of a nine year period. This is the equivalent of an 8 percent compound annual interest rate. If the annuity had a 2 percent term yield spread this would be deducted from the annual interest rate (8 percent-2 percent) and the net rate would be credited to the contract (6 percent) for each of the nine years. Total index gain may also be computed by using the highest anniversary index level as the end point.

VARIABLE ANNUITY – A contract issued by an insurance company offering separate accounts invested in a wide variety of stocks and/or bonds. The investment risk is borne by the annuity owner. Variable annuities are considered securities and require appropriate securities registration.

1035 EXCHANGE – The 1035 exchange refers to the section of tax code that allows annuity owners the flexibility to exchange one annuity for another without incurring any immediate tax liabilities. This action is most often utilized when an annuity holder decides they want to upgrade an annuity to a more favorable one, but they do not want to activate unnecessary tax liabilities that would typically be encountered when surrendering an existing annuity contract.

401(K) ROLLOVER – SEE IRA ROLLOVER

Made in the USA
Monee, IL
29 May 2023